DAVID BADDIEL is a writer in London. He is also, would you believe, a Jew.

Praise for

Jews Don't Count

"*Jews Don't Count* is a supreme piece of reasoning and passionate, yet controlled, argument. From his first sentence, the energy, force and conviction of Baddiel's writing and thinking will transfix you ... as readable as an airport thriller ... a masterpiece." STEPHEN FRY

"I don't think I have ever been so grateful to anyone for writing a book. Baddiel's *Jews Don't Count* is incisive, urgent, surprisingly funny and short. It's also a beautiful piece of publishing. It needs to be read." JAY RAYNER

"Brilliant, furious, uncomfortable, funny. Essential reading." SIMON MAYO

"I'm about a quarter of the way into this thus far and it's very well argued and written. It's a book you know the author HAD to write, and those are the best books."

JON RONSON

Jews Don't Count

Also by David Baddiel

The Death of Eli Gold
The Secret Purposes
Whatever Love Means
Time for Bed

(The Boy Who Got) Accidentally Famous
Future Friend
The Taylor Turbochaser
Head Kid
Birthday Boy
AniMalcolm
The Boy Who Could Do What He Liked
The Person Controller
The Parent Agency

Jews Don't Count

*How Identity Politics
Failed One Particular Identity*

David Baddiel

TLS

TLS Books
An imprint of HarperCollins*Publishers*
1 London Bridge Street
London SE1 9GF

The-TLS.co.uk

HarperCollins*Publishers*
1st Floor, Watermarque Building, Ringsend Road
Dublin 4, Ireland

First published in Great Britain in 2021 by TLS Books
First published in the United States in 2021 by TLS Books
This TLS paperback edition published in 2022

23 24 25 26 27 LBC 9 8 7 6 5

Image on p. 52 reproduced by permission of
The Times/News Licensing

A catalogue record for this book is
available from the British Library

ISBN 978-0-00-853019-8

Typeset in Publico Text
Printed and bound in the USA by Lakeside Book Company

MIX
Paper from
responsible sources
FSC™ C007454

This book is produced from independently certified FSC™ paper
to ensure responsible forest management.

For more information visit: www.harpercollins.co.uk/green

To my mother, Sarah Fabian-Baddiel,
who never failed to make herself count.

Jews Don't Count

Preface

This is a preface to make this book more appealing to the American reader, so I may as well start with a very American reference. In Season 1, Episode 1 of *The West Wing*, there is a scene in which an irate Christian evangelical group go to the White House to register an official complaint about some moral failing they feel has been exhibited by the fictional administration. The tactic of the White House aides is to mollify them, but this goes wrong when a particularly angry woman on the evangelical side makes a slighting reference to one of the aides having what she calls a "New York sense of humor." The conversation continues for a short while, but then the character Toby Ziegler says: "She meant Jewish." The woman indignantly refutes this, but of course we, the viewers, know that Toby, and the writer, Aaron Sorkin, are correct. They are correct, that is, that antisemitism is a racism that often shows itself in codes and tropes and assumptions. It is, as one antiracist tweeter said, after being shocked at how unwittingly snared he had been by some of the traps outlined in this book, "the racism that sneaks past you." *Jews Don't Count* is to some extent a primer to prevent that sneakiness, to spot the traps in advance: perhaps even to see when you yourself—and by you, I'm imagining you, the reader of this book, not as a hardline religious fundamentalist like the woman in *The West Wing*, but as a reasonably progressive person concerned with fighting discrimination in all its forms—have fallen into them.

I am an American, Troy, in New York state, born. But my parents were British—well, Welsh and German, to be exact—and brought me back to the U.K. when I was three months old, so although I have a U.S. passport, I can't really claim, in my soul, to be a real Yank.* Which is why, after this book came out in the U.K., it was felt that I needed to tweak it a bit for the American reader.

The job of doing so was partly the usual "divided by a common language" one. That was fairly easy: there are definitely no references in this edition left to grills, aubergines or fannies. Political references required a little more work. This book was to some extent catalyzed by the five years in which Jeremy Corbyn was leader of the U.K. Labour Party, and it's worth knowing, as you perhaps may not, that his tenure was marked by

---

* I don't even know, for example, whether Americans really still use the word Yank.

allegations of antisemitism that swirled around both him and the new larger membership that joined the party on his coronation—allegations that led antisemitism to have a much greater visibility and presence in the British political conversation than at any time since World War Two. But you don't need to be acquainted with every detail about that, not least because the issue of how antisemitism plays out, both consciously and unconsciously, in left-leaning discourse, stretches back far longer, and far wider, geographically, culturally, and psychologically, than that single political moment.

I have tried, nonetheless, to fix or footnote any reference points not immediately accessible to a non-U.K. reader. Beyond this, there is one greater complexity, which points to the heart of what this book is about. It is the project of this polemic to shine a light on the ways in which the progressive consensus has failed, in a time of deep intensification of concern about discrimination faced by minorities in general, to apply that concern to Jews, and the discrimination they suffer. Doing that involves calling that discrimination what I have already called it, and what it is: racism. It is absolutely at the heart of this book that antisemitism is racism.

A refusal to accept that antisemitism is racism comes, obviously, from the racists, who refuse to accept that most racisms are racism. But this book is really for anti-racists, or at least, those who would claim to be so. In the U.K., the acknowledgment that antisemitism is racism, among the antiracist community, has involved some shift of perception, and it is my argument that among those who do acknowledge it, there is an underlying sense that it is not *real* racism, or that it is a lesser form. Beyond that, however, there are those, Jews included, and I perceive this to be more prevalent in the U.S., who resist the classification of antisemitism as racism for more complex reasons. There is a notion out there that identifying antisemitism as racism, and therefore of Jews as a race, or an ethnicity, has negative echoes, given a history in which Nazis insisted on that classification for obviously very bad reasons.

But although this is a book in which that history is given great weight, and consideration as alive in the psychological present, it is my contention that such logic makes no sense, or certainly not anymore. The Nazis imposed those conditions on Jews at a time when ideas of identity and representation, for any ethnicity apart from White European, hardly existed. In contrast, presently, much of the power of antiracism comes from an insistence on those things: on being identified and represented. This can be seen from the 2021 census in the U.K. In an effort to represent, and to include, the ethnicity boxes offered included three different Black categories, five Asian (split into east and south), a number of mixed-race white, Black, and Asian options, Gypsy, Traveler, white Irish, and many others.

Given that many of these ethnicities were also targeted by the Nazis, the "but classifying us as an ethnicity is what the Third Reich did" argument doesn't hold up: it doesn't hold up because we live in a time—luckily—when ethnicity is something to be celebrated, not hidden. It is indeed a key part of the struggle against discrimination that this is so. But meanwhile, on the 2021 U.K. census, there was no ethnicity box for Jews. Not even—I have to say I thought this might just have occurred to the form-creators via word association—after the listing for Arab. Jews were relegated to the Other box.

Jewish *was* offered, as an option, in the religion category. I discuss the confusion between Jewishness and Judaism in this book, and don't wish in this preface to present spoilers, but suffice it to say that as an atheist, like many Jews, I could not tick that box. Which means that for those who would suggest that Jewish should not be considered a race or an ethnicity, I am not a Jew. This is—to use an English term which I'm not going to translate for American ears—bollocks. The religion, in terms of the discussion of how to fight antisemitism, is virtually irrelevant. To fight antisemitism, you have to be aware of how the antisemites see Jewishness, which is as a thing in your blood, not your spiritual soul.

The endpoint of this idea was presented to me recently by a Jewish Labour Party member, who told me that during the Corbyn years, a pamphlet purporting to be educating members about the Holocaust was circulating at one of the party conferences. It listed, apparently, all the groups targeted by the Nazis, including disabled people, gays, Roma, and political prisoners. The one group it didn't mention was Jews. The principal target of the Nazis did not feature. When the member made a complaint about this, he was told exactly what those who would refute the idea of Jewish ethnicity say: why are you accepting a classification placed upon you by the Nazis? These are just *white Europeans* who were killed. Which means that the eventual conclusion of that argument is Holocaust denial.

The thing is, as far as ethnicity goes, I don't have a choice. Those who say "why accept what the Nazis would classify you as?" have never really had to imagine being forced at gunpoint onto a cattle truck. It's incredibly simplistic to think that, as a minority, our sense of ourselves should not include how, over the years, we've been thought of by the racists. My sense of Jewishness as an ethnicity is to some extent about what Nazis did to us. Of course it is. It's not just about that—it's about many positive things, as well—but the way that positive and negative associations combine to create minority identity is complex. Identity, particularly ethnic identity, is created in the story of survival against the odds, which is why the blues are songs of sadness, and fightback, and celebration, all mixed up. That's what identity is. If you want to see both the negative and positive merged as one, think of the old joke that Jews tell each other about how you can boil down all Jewish festivals to a simple mantra: they tried to kill us, they failed, let's eat. That is the Jewish blues, and we should all sing it.

Which brings us back to America, and this edition. We live in a time of great redress around minorities, no more so than in the U.S. Part of this has involved a new concept, coming out of this country: one of allyship. There is an urge, particularly among progressives, to be allies—to be trans allies, or Black allies, or gay allies; whichever minority might be seen to be in need of a helping hand, it will be offered. Jews, as Sarah Silverman has said recently, prompted by this book, have a history of allyship with other minorities: they have indeed provided that helping hand. But, as she also said, where are the Jewish allies? You don't, it is true, see many posts on Twitter or Instagram making that claim. The sense, perhaps, is that Jews don't need allies. That isn't true: it never was. And my hope is that *Jews Don't Count* may lead to a few more.

I'm going to give you some examples of a recurring phenomenon. My publisher here is the *Times Literary Supplement*, so let's begin with a literary one. In August 2020, the British newspaper the *Observer*, which, along with its sister paper the *Guardian*, is politically the most progressive mainstream news outlet in the country, published a review of the screenwriter Charlie Kaufman's first novel *Antkind*. It wasn't a very positive review, criticizing the book mainly because the narrator operates from what the critic calls a "white-male-cis-het perspective." In other words self-evidently white, male, and, less self-evidently, possessed of a gender that is neither trans nor non-binary, and a sexuality that is straight. Anyone occupying this square of characteristics is considered, by those who assume that all social structures are underpinned by power, privileged. White-male-cis-hets have four head starts in life. A book written from a white-male-cis-het perspective would routinely be marked down by a platform like the *Observer*, keen always to re-center the cultural conversation away from that square.

However, the narrator in *Antkind* is called B. Rosenberger Rosenberg. He describes himself early on as having a "rabbinical" beard, as "Jewish-looking"; perhaps even more of a giveaway, at one point he wears a tie with the slogan "100% Kosher." There are numerous occasions when other characters behave antisemitically toward him, assuming his behaviors tally with Jewish stereo-types, whispering "Jew" under their breath as he leaves rooms, or shouting "Fuck you, Hebrew!" directly at him. But in the *Observer* review, there's no mention of his Jewishness, or the issue of Jewishness in the book in general, despite it including—thank you, Kindle—sixty mentions of the word "Jew," and ninety of the word "Jewish." And, of course, Charlie Kaufman himself is Jewish.

But I guess none of this, for the *Observer* critic, has any bearing on B. Rosenberger Rosenberg's white-male-cis-het perspective: no bearing, that is, on his privilege.

Here is another example, this time from the Danish comedian Sofie Hagen. In a—very good—2019 short film she made about body positivity, Hagen recites a list of "the most oppressed people in society," a list that includes: "Black people and people of color, queer people, trans people, Muslims, and people with disabilities." Which indeed is a pretty good stab at covering the waterfront of what many progressives would consider to be the most oppressed groups, the most persecuted minorities, in society.

But it misses out one persecuted minority, one of the most persecuted minorities in history. Now. Imagine that the main character in *Antkind* belonged to any of these minorities that Hagen mentions. The central premise of the *Observer* review—that the problematic issue with *Antkind* is that it is written from a white-male-cis-het perspective—would dissolve, and with it, most of the review's negativity. Which means that despite the history of persecution, there is only one minority that, for the privilege-checkers, stays firmly in the square of privilege.

Time for a high literary example: on New Year's Day 2017, BBC Radio 4* broadcast Jeremy Irons reading from the complete collection of T.S. Eliot's poems, almost in their entirety. Anyone who knows Eliot's poetry will know that reading all of his poems means the inevitable inclusion of these lines from "Gerontion":

---

* Radio 4 is the flagship BBC radio speech station. Its brand, despite some recent attempts to streetwise it up a bit, is erudite. It's where you'll find, along with news and comedy, programs about Albrecht Dürer, and Bertolt Brecht, and William Gladstone. It's probably the place, still, where the BBC is at its most BBC-ish.

My house is a decayed house,
And the Jew squats on the window sill, the owner,
Spawned in some estaminet of Antwerp,
Blistered in Brussels, patched and peeled in
     London.

And from "Burbank with a Baedeker: Bleistein with a Cigar":

The rats are underneath the piles.
The Jew is underneath the lot.

I remember listening, and wondering how the BBC would get round this. When it came to these particular poems, they enlisted the help of Anthony Julius, a Jewish lawyer, and the author of *T.S. Eliot, Anti-Semitism and Literary Form* (1995), who prefaced the readings with his theory of how the highly prevalent, fashionable antisemitism of the time informed and possibly even enhanced Eliot's work. To simplify considerably, Julius believes that Eliot was such a great poet that he could—almost uniquely, although there is of course *The Merchant of Venice*—make antisemitism into art.

I wrote to Anthony Julius after this because I think his position is wrong. I'm an Eliot fan, but I think the poetry does not redeem the hatred. We ended up some time later having lunch and talking about it for three hours (a very, if I might say so, Jewish reaction to the whole thing).

But none of this shook off the feeling I had, on New Year's Day 2017, that, however great the writer, however great the writing, no other minority group would be compared to rats, or envisaged as any similar negative racist stereotype, on Radio 4. It is not inconceivable that the BBC might read a whole Agatha Christie book on New Year's Day. It is, however, inconceivable that anyone will hear Jeremy Irons' voice saying, "And now, *Ten Little N****rs*."

Meanwhile, in mid-2020, following the spate of statues being toppled as part of the Black Lives Matter protests, a protester a long way from Minneapolis—in Broadstairs, Kent, in southern England—sprayed the words "Dickens Was A Racist" on the Dickens Museum. The protester was called Ian Driver and his inspiration was a letter that Dickens had written in 1857 decrying the Indian Mutiny, an uprising against the colonial rule of the British East India Company. Unquestionably, the letter is racist. However, it is strange that Ian Driver had to go all the way to a relatively obscure piece of writing by Dickens to become inflamed by his racism, when, in *Oliver Twist*, in plain sight, for years and years and years, has been Fagin.

But maybe he doesn't count.

* * *

The modern cultural conversation about reassessing great writers from the past in the light of current political understanding is not always, however, negative. In the case, for example, of the early twentieth-century novelist Edith Wharton, that reassessment has recently been about upping her status in the canon, with a sense that, as a woman, she had been overlooked. In the latter part of 2020, the *Guardian*'s online reading group chose Wharton's *The Age of Innocence* as its book for September. Meanwhile, in the politically more conservative but still culturally progressive *The Times*, Anna Murphy wrote of her love for *The House of Mirth*, and specifically about how pleased she was that Wharton was finally being recognized as "a match" for Henry James.

It's certainly the case that with some notable excep-tions, women authors have not been given their due by the culture, so this re-evaluation of Wharton made me decide to pick up *The House of Mirth*. I was very much enjoying the heroine Lily Bart's adventures in the first few pages, until a character called Mr. Rosedale—"a little Jew who had been served up and rejected on the social board a dozen times within her reminiscence ..."*—is introduced. The issue is not, of course, that Wharton, in

---

* The narrator continues: "He had his race's accuracy in the appraisal of values, and to be seen walking down the platform at the crowded afternoon hour in the company of Miss Lily Bart would have been money in his pocket, as he might himself have phrased it."

her time and context, wrote things that we would now consider to be antisemitic. The issue is that this is not a problem for her present feminist reclamation. Meanwhile, other types of racism that her writing might express continue, for some, to be. In an essay for the feminist website Jezebel, the Victorian literary scholar Rachel Vorona Cote writes: "Excluding what Wharton's characters—or, for that matter, Wharton herself—might have to say about my Jewish family, my whiteness supplies me with a pair of cozy blinkers that occlude the tarnishing details. Once I turn my attention to the novel's treatment of persons of color—peripheral, dismissive—I cannot regain my uncomplicated enjoyment of it."

It's good that Vorona Cote is interrogating Wharton's assumptions. If I was to interrogate her own, the question I would ask is: why exclude what Wharton's characters or Wharton herself would say about Jews?

Here's another example.

In 2019, a production of *The Color Purple,* based on Alice Walker's novel, was due to be staged as a musical in London. About four weeks before it opened, the actress who was going to be playing the starring role of Celie, Seyi Omooba, was found to have posted—in 2014— homophobic messages on Facebook. Omooba is from an evangelical Christian background, and her posts were fairly standard evangelical Christian messages about the sinfulness of same-sex activity. She refused to apologize for them and was fired.

I'm not interested, for the purposes of this book, in the overall rights and wrongs of cancel culture. But what is important, for the purposes of this book, is that Omooba *was* canceled, at least as far as the show was concerned, for homophobia.

Alice Walker published in 2017 a poem called "To Study The Talmud." The Talmud is a book of exegesis of the Old Testament, codified in the fourteenth century and containing the basis of all the archaic rules and laws of Judaism: it was written mainly by rabbis. It has been misquoted extensively by antisemites wishing to suggest that Jews drink Christian blood and promote pedophilia. Here's what Walker wrote:

> Are Goyim (us) meant to be slaves of Jews, and not
>   only
> That, but to enjoy it?
> Are three year old (and a day) girls eligible for
>   marriage and intercourse?
> Are young boys fair game for rape?
> Must even the best of the Goyim (us, again) be
>   killed?
> Pause a moment and think what this could mean
> Or already has meant
> In our own lifetime.

Walker, like Omooba, has used ancient religion to uphold and promote stereotypes and discrimination against a minority group. Omooba says: "It is clearly evident in I Corinthians vi, 9-11 what the Bible says on this matter. I do not believe you can be born gay, and I do not believe homosexual practice is right." This is an anti-gay position. Walker says: Jews believe that pedophilia, slavery, and the murder of non-Jews are sanctioned by their religion. This is an anti-Jewish position. It is also, I would suggest, the more powerfully expressed of the two positions ("I do not believe" is a statement of opinion; "Jews believe" is a statement of—incorrect—fact). Omooba got canceled. Alice Walker—no one ever even suggested she should be. And, of course, *The Color Purple* musical went ahead.

We live in heightened times, politically. When I was growing up, in the 1970s and 1980s, it was a mantra that the personal was political, but even so, now, the politicization of all things, on the back of identity politics driven by social media, puts that time in the shade. This was evident in a recent documentary on BBC TV, about the drama strand *Play for Today*. *Play for Today*, which ran from 1970 to 1984, was a showcase for single plays on television, and was a breeding ground for many significant British dramatists. My memory of those plays was that they were very varied in tone and subject matter, but this documentary, which was called "Drama Out of a

Crisis," highlighted only those that expressed radical politics and social issues. It made a point, therefore, of focusing on the few plays in the *Play for Today* strand that dealt with minorities, notably the work of Black writer and director Horace Ové, but also the one play that, ahead of its time—although in tune with ours—dealt with transgender issues.

In 1977, on *Play for Today*, the BBC screened Jack Rosenthal's play *Bar Mitzvah Boy*. It won that year's BAFTA for best single play. Two years earlier, *Play for Today* had screened Rosenthal's *The Evacuees*, a drama about two Jewish children forced to live with non-Jewish foster parents during World War Two. It also won a BAFTA, and an international Emmy. But more importantly for me, as a young teenager in London, both of these plays were the first real example of representation of my life, on TV. They were the first time I had seen the British-Jewish experience accurately portrayed anywhere in the culture.

In "Drama Out of a Crisis," neither of these plays were mentioned.

Sometimes, you hear what I'm talking about out loud. The major BBC current affairs show, the one that sets the news agenda every morning, is the *Today* program on Radio 4. It's a must-listen for those interested in politics. And a must-react to: if something controversial is said on

Today, Twitter is set alight, and the conversation explodes.

On March 13, 2019, the American pollster John Zogby was on. At one point, he began talking about fissures in the Democratic Party, specifically around the then new Congresswoman Ilhan Omar's views about Israel and its supporters in the U.S. The interviewer, Justin Webb, who is a regular on *Today*, said, in response:

> If the party decided to say to its supporters, "Look, we think that antisemitism is a bit like the way some of our people might regard anti-white racism, that actually it's a different order of racism. It's not as important—it's still bad—but it's not as important as some other forms of racism," what impact do you think that might have?

It was a strange moment. It felt less like a question and more like a helpful suggestion. *Maybe this would be a way forward for the Democrats?* was the tone. Webb did not qualify or contextualize it. He did not preface or add "Obviously this is offensive to say, but perhaps it's what some people in the party actually think." His tone was neutral.

Zogby moved on without really answering. But even if he had, it was the question itself I was struck by. I remember listening and thinking, Blimey, it's rare that someone just comes out with it: *Antisemitism is a second-class racism*. I thought it would create controversy. I thought that there would be an intense reaction.

There wasn't. Well, that's not true. There was a bit, after I managed, following much fiddling about with the BBC radio online player and recording devices on my computer, to record the question and post it on Twitter, along with a sense of my amazement. Even then, there wasn't that much online noise, and what noise there was came mainly from Jews.*

So actually, when I say "Sometimes you hear it out loud," what I really heard was the silence.

An example from my sporting life. In 2008, I was sitting, as usual on a Saturday afternoon, with my brother Ivor watching Chelsea FC at their home ground, Stamford Bridge. This is the football—OK, U.S. readers, soccer—team we support. We'd been going for many years, and by this point sat in the Upper East Stand. Chelsea were playing another Premier League club, Aston Villa. The game was dull. On the big screen, a score came up of another match. Chelsea's London rivals Tottenham

---

* One thing that did happen is that Justin Webb got in touch with me privately to make it clear that however it sounded, his intention was not to condone such an idea, or present it as a genuine way forward, but to suggest only that it exists as a way of thinking for many in the Democratic Party.

Hotspur were being beaten by a considerably less glamorous club, Hull.

The bored crowd picked up on this and started chanting "We hate Tottenham, and we hate Tottenham." Then, with wearying predictability, this mutated into the crowd chanting the word "Yiddo." For those who don't know about this phenomenon, the Tottenham Hotspur football club (known as Spurs) is located in an area of London that is fairly well populated by Jews. For this reason, Spurs fans both self-identify and are identified by others as a "Jewish" club—even though the vast majority of them aren't Jewish—and this leads to various chants based around the word "Yid." Those who do know about it are still generally confused, as they tend to think it's all just Spurs fans chanting this word "positively." It isn't. It is also chanted by the fans of Chelsea, Arsenal, West Ham, and other clubs *at* Spurs fans, menacingly, horribly, along with associated antisemitic chants—"Spurs are on their way to Auschwitz," for example—and hissing to simulate the noise of gas chambers.

On this particular afternoon, the chanting of the word "Yiddo" was joined by one particular fan about ten rows behind us deciding to shout, repeatedly, "Fuck the fucking Yids! Fuck the fucking Yids!" And then, just to make clear that, by Yids, he didn't just mean "Spurs fans," that became "Fuck the fucking Jews! Fuck the fucking Jews!" This went on for some time. Me and Ivor looked at each other. Ivor said: "What should we do?" I shrugged. So then my brother, bless him, got up, turned round and told the bloke to shut up. The man replied, in the classic mode, "No, you fucking shut up." Ivor said, "No, you fucking shut up." And then, miraculously, he did. The racist shut up. Ivor sat down and said, "I think I'm going to cry."

By the time this happened, we had sat—well, stood and then sat—listening to this stuff at Stamford Bridge for thirty years. Over that period the culture around racism in football changed immeasurably. In the 1970s, football fandom was unbelievably racist, and immense strides were made to eradicate it over the next decades by organizations like Kick It Out. By 2008, the world had definitely moved on. So much so that the Chelsea program that day contained a very clear message that any racist abuse heard in the stands at matches would lead to immediate intervention by stewards and a life-ban for the abuser concerned.

Well, not *any* racist abuse, it turns out. No steward intervened when this happened; and no life-ban was imposed on the man shouting "Fuck the fucking Jews." The world had moved on. But it seems that it had forgotten something; it had left one racism behind.

When people talk about antisemitism, what they tend to mean is an active process. They mean a specific targeted attack, such as Nazis or white supremacists describing

Jews as vermin or responsible for all the world's evil. Antisemitism, in most people's minds, puts Jews right in the middle of the sniper's sights. But what I've begun with here is a series of examples of the opposite: of absences. Of something—a concern, a protectiveness, a championing, a cry for increased visibility, whatever it might be—*not* being applied to Jews. Sofie Hagen's list of the most oppressed people in society was one example of that absence, and at the U.K. Labour Party conference in 2019, Dawn Butler, the Shadow Secretary of State for Women and Equalities, presented a supercharged version of it. In a rousing close to her speech, Butler listed all the people who might be considered to be outside the mainstream of society whom the Labour Party would value, and protect from discrimination:

> If you are in social housing, if you are LGBT+, if you are straight, if you are a traveler, if you struggle to pay rent, if you wear a hijab, turban, a cross, if you are Black, white, Asian, if you are disabled, if you don't have a trust fund, if you didn't go to Oxbridge,* if you are working class, if you are under eighteen, if you are aspirational, if you work, if you are a carer, if you feel you won't live beyond twenty-five,

---

* A contraction of Oxford or Cambridge University. People who go to these universities are assumed—sometimes correctly, sometimes not—to be privileged.

if you have ever ticked the other box—you have a future and you are worthy, worthy of equality, dignity, and respect. And a Labour government will value you, just be your true authentic self.

This list is slightly odd in that it includes a number of categories that would already be considered mainstream, including "white' and "straight," but maybe Butler was very keen not to alienate anyone in this particular speech. Not to leave *any* group out.

But she did.

This book is not an exhaustive account of modern anti-semitism. Those exist elsewhere. But it is going to be an attempt to pinpoint something that I think is key to modern antisemitism, which is the left's confusion over it. By the left, what I really mean is progressives: the coalition—some of whom may not be classically left-wing—of those who would define themselves as being *on the right side of history*. I'm not sure this is a phrase used that much outside of online discourse, but it denotes those who stand against all -isms and phobias—racism, sexism, ableism, Islamophobia, transphobia—and who believe that in the future those -isms and phobias will be recognized as clearly aberrant, and consigned to time's trashcan. I should make it clear that the phrase "all -isms and phobias" is not meant to be patronizing or belittling, it's just a shorthand for what I'm trying to say. I would define myself as progressive. Although I never use the phrase "on the right side of history," as I believe the only person who really knows how things will turn out in years to come is Doctor Who.

It's important that this is clear: this book is about progressives. Progressives themselves will sometimes respond to antisemitism by pointing to the—implied— much worse racism suffered by other minorities in, say, opinion columns in the right-wing *Daily Mail*. A fair enough point, but I'm not interested in those columnists, as their racism is active and obvious, and also, to be honest, not mine to talk about. I want to talk about anti-semitism and, most importantly, the antisemitism that needs to be deconstructed, which blatant far-right anti-Jewish statements do not. What we have looked at so far are examples of Jews being left out: left out, by the left, of identity politics. Identity politics, for anyone who doesn't know, is a politics whereby traditional things that the left and right fight about—basically economics—get surpassed by issues like racism, and disablism, and homophobia. The duty of the left becomes less about supporting the working man (although many left thinkers would say that economic injustice goes hand in hand with injustices perpetrated against minorities, which I agree with) and more about the championing of people of color, and gays, and trans people—all the people named by Dawn Butler. This is the good fight, and the left is always a fight-y space, defined by its rebelliousness.

I use the phrase "good fight" advisedly. The left have always thought of themselves as the good guys. I lean politically toward the left (as a teen, I was going to Young Communist meetings) and so I can't really speak for the right, but it seems to me that people on the right are less bothered about a virtuous self-image. You can be a Conservative and happily believe that human nature, as suggested by capitalist economics, is rampantly self-interested, and because this creates free societies which in times of plenty function well, if unequally, then that's fine. Which means that you don't have to project yourself, and your politics, continually onto the moral high ground. The left are fighty, because they are the outsiders. The right are the Establishment, which makes the left the rebels, the mavericks, the revolutionaries (although this language was in recent years appropriated by Donald Trump and Brexiteers, but that really is another story).

With the transition to identity politics the left's cause has become fragmented. It has become less about fighting for the masses and more about specific minorities. The good fight is for all the people mentioned by Dawn Butler. Butler's speech formed the soundtrack to the Labour Party's last big campaign video before the 2019 general election, one in which the question of the prevalence of antisemitism in Labour under its then leader

Jeremy Corbyn played a significant part. Which meant that all these various groups who the Labour Party was pledging to fight for were present and correct in the visuals, and the exclusion, or forgetting, of Jews from this sacred circle was hammered home.

A sacred circle is drawn around those whom the progressive modern left are prepared to go into battle for, and it seems as if the Jews aren't in it. Why? Well, there are lots of answers. But the basic one, underpinning all others, is that Jews are the only objects of racism who are imagined—by the racists—as both low and high status. Jews are stereotyped, by the racists, in all the same ways that other minorities are—as lying, thieving, dirty, vile, stinking—but *also* as moneyed, privileged, powerful, and secretly in control of the world. Jews are somehow both sub-human and humanity's secret masters. And it's this racist mythology that's in the air when the left pause before putting Jews into their sacred circle. Because all the people in the sacred circle are *oppressed*. And if you believe, even a little bit, that Jews are moneyed, privileged, powerful, and secretly in control of the world ... well, you can't put them into the sacred circle of the oppressed. Some might even say they belong in the damned circle of the oppressors.

One way of illustrating these submerged ideas about Jews is through food. Food, now, is a culture-war battleground. The cultural appropriation of food—the usage of recipes and ideas originating from minority cultures by, predominantly, white western chefs and restaurateurs—is a much-debated subject among progressives, and there are many, like the journalist and food blogger Ruth Tam, who have written about how (in her case in the United States) "immigrant food is often treated like discount tourism—a cheap means for foodies to feel worldly without leaving the comfort of their neighborhood—or high-minded fusion—a stylish way for American chefs to use other cultures' cuisines to reap profit." If you Google "cultural appropriation food" you'll find much more on this subject, and if you want to dig into it, add to your search window, "Chinese," or "Indian," or "Caribbean," for specific examples of concern and anger. As an experiment, I added the word "Jewish." Despite the—not mythic, completely true—fact that Jews are obsessed with food, and despite the appropriation of bagels, chopped liver, schmaltz herring, chicken soup, and salt beef by many, many non-Jewish outlets, particularly in America, I found not a single blogpost or newspaper article or tweet complaining about this, or even simply identifying it as a thing. I did find some search results, of course. They were articles angrily accusing Jews, Israelis to be specific, of appropriating Palestinian food. Jews, in other words, even in the left-field arena of recipe stealing, are identified as the stealers, not the stolen from: the oppressors, not the victims.

Surely, though, progressives don't believe all those racist myths about Jews? Well. Here is an image retweeted in 2019 by the actor and activist John Cusack.

This is a common meme on social media. The quote is attributed to Voltaire—who, indeed, was antisemitic, thinking that Jews were too "Asiatic" ever to integrate into Europe and "deserved to be punished" for that failure—but really, he's just there to give the words a spurious legitimacy. In fact the quote comes from Kevin Strom, an American white supremacist and neo-Nazi, and it shows the key element of such utterances: defiance. The reason far-right and progressive left activists might conjoin over this idea of fighting back against mythical, sacrosanct secret rulers is that both like to see themselves as rebels, as fighters against power, and Jews, uniquely among minorities in the west, are associated with power.

The difference between progressives and the far right can be summed up in two words: Cusack apologized. The importance of that is not so much the fact of apology, but that in apologizing, Cusack, who said that he "did not have an antisemitic bone in his body," acknowledged the existence of a blind spot. This comes back to what I said earlier about the difference between the active quality of traditional far-right anti-Jewish racism and the passive nature of the progressive neglect of Jewish sensibilities. But at what point does that neglect— given that we live in a time when almost any microaggression against a minority can be flagged as racism—shade back into racism? How macro does an aggression against Jews have to be to be seen as an aggression? To not realize that the image Cusack retweeted is clearly and violently antisemitic is—well, it's really quite a big blind spot.

Cusack is not alone, though, in needing a Jewish rearview mirror. After that incident at Chelsea in 2008, me and my brother, having failed to get any traction at all from the club in tracking down the racist abuser and punishing him, decided to make a short film, called *The Y-Word*. *The Y-Word* is a two-minute piece, which went online but was also shown at stadiums before games. In it various famous soccer players (including Frank Lampard, Ledley King, and others) pointed out that other words—the N-word and the P-word*—were no longer heard at football grounds: so why was the Y-word?

There are a number of things that are worth mentioning in passing here. The film was hard to get made. We went first of all to the already-mentioned antiracist football campaigning organization Kick It Out. Their attitude was entirely doubtful. Their basic position was: does this

---

* I'm told by my U.S. editor that "P-word" needs an explainer. This is a conceptual problem, as the whole point of calling a hate word by the usage "X-word" is to avoid saying or printing the offensive word in full. So I'm not going to do that in a footnote either. But for anyone confused, I am referring to a hate word commonly applied in the U.K. to Pakistanis, and indeed often also to Brown people not of that heritage.

really matter? There was still abuse going on from the terrace toward Black players, and they had a campaign about to start on homophobia. Won't a campaign about antisemitism defocus the more important messages? In fact, the basic sense that—let me say it here for the first time—Jews don't count meant that for a long time it looked like the film wasn't going to get made until, amazingly, Gary Lineker, an ex-Spurs player, agreed to take part.

Also, the Y-word. There's a reason we called it that, because, actually, despite all the furor that the film caused about whether or not Tottenham Hotspur fans had the right to self-identify as Yids, it was not really about football. It was trying to question why there is not a level playing field around racism. Why some racisms seem to be thought of as more important—more offensive, more troubling, more in need of being shut down— than others. If there was a club from a part of London that was thought of as predominantly Black, and the mainly white fanbase of that club decided to call themselves the N-words, or the N-word army, and that led to opposing fans chanting racist hate songs based around the N-word back at them, it would be stopped and the club shut down immediately. So by calling the film *The Y-Word*, we were saying maybe the hate words for Jews— and Yid is one, daubed as it was across London's traditionally Jewish East End by Oswald Mosley's blackshirts in fascist marches before World War Two—need to be considered as equally unmentionable as the hate words for other ethnic minorities.

But you'll notice that in the last paragraph, I did just write the word "Yid" in full. And I have already, in this book, written it out. I would not do that with the P-word, and certainly not the N-word. Which suggests a hierarchy of offense: a hierarchy that exists even now, even in this book that I'm writing. Yid is considered *not as bad* hate speech as the P-word or the N-word.

The film led to much debate, and at one point the then Prime Minister David Cameron weighed in saying that he thought it was OK for Spurs fans to "call themselves Yids." Forget the spurious argument about OK-ness. Consider the fact that he was just *fine* to say the word, to let it pass his lips. And how un-fine he would be to do so with the P-word or the N-word.*

---

* A small addendum: a little while after David Cameron said this, I was on an ITV politics debate show called *The Agenda*. Cameron, having realized that I was on the show with him, was still worried. He walked into the green room, came straight for me and said: "Are we going to be talking about the Yid thing?" He then told me he'd thought about it, or rather spoken to his advisor Lord Feldman about it, and Lord Feldman had said "Baddiel is right" and the prime minister had decided to go with that. Although not to the point of actually understanding that casually using the word Yid—in this case, in front of a Jew—might be a bad thing. He was still not bothered, at all, about saying Yid out loud. In front of a Jew. (I was tempted to say "In front of a Yid" then, for comedy, but that would really not help my point.)

This very subject—the inequity of offense that right-thinking people take around differing hate words—came up when a friend of mine, a man who very much would be thought of as a progressive, questioned me about this central premise of the film. He said: but the Y-word *isn't* as bad as the N-word? I said: why not? He said: *because Jews are rich.*

It still seems to me an amazing thing for an avowed antiracist to say (not least because of its implicit assumption that Black people can never be rich). What my friend was saying is that because Jews are—come on, we all know they are—comfortable, privileged, and moneyed, they don't need, not really, the protections of antiracism, the ones most promoted by the left.

Perhaps it's not that amazing. Some on the left, inspired by Marxist thought, would agree. The journalist Ash Sarkar, who is a communist, said in 2018, while writing a *Guardian* column against the acceptance of the International Holocaust Remembrance Alliance's definition of antisemitism, that "This is where we must think very seriously about what the work of antiracism is. Antisemitism, at this point in history, is primarily experienced as prejudice and hostility towards Jews as Jews, largely without aspects of material dispossession (such as structural unemployment) that manifest in other forms of racism. Islamophobia and racialised xenophobia has a much greater proximity to shaping policy, particularly

related to immigration, integration and criminal justice."*
The suggestion here is that, because Jews *are* materially
better off—I'm not sure what else "without aspects of
material dispossession" means—than other ethnic
minorities, it *is* a lesser form of racism. It all comes down
to money.

Well. First, it is always dangerous, however cleverly
you word it, to say Jews are rich. Jews *aren't* rich,
particularly. Some are. And some aren't. A study by the
non-partisan wealth research firm New World Wealth
found that 56.2 percent of the 13.1 million millionaires in
the world were Christian, while 6.5 percent were Muslim,
3.9 percent were Hindu, and 1.7 percent were Jewish. In
the U.S., 48 percent of Hindus have a yearly household
income of $100,000 or more, and 70 percent have at
least $75,000, which makes them the highest-earning
ethnic group.

But either way—and this is very un-Marxist of me—
fuck off about money. Because money doesn't protect
you from racism. As I say, some Jews *are* rich. My

---

* It's important to note that Sarkar, who I consider one of the most
eloquent progressive writers working today, also says, in the same
article: "Jews are once again being painted as rootless cosmopolitans
and subverters of democracy in Europe ... Such tropes are part of a
wider project to use idea of the 'enemy within' to break and remake
society in the image of increasingly hardline ethnonationalism.
Antisemitic hate crime in the U.K. is at an all-time high. The left
cannot afford any complacency."

grandparents were: they were industrialists in East Prussia. They owned a brick factory. They had servants. By the time they were fleeing to England with my mother as a baby in 1939, however, that had all been robbed from them. And by the end of the war, most of their family—and therefore a large section of mine—had been murdered. It doesn't matter how rich you are, because the racists will smash in the door of your big house that they know you don't deserve anyway and *only own because you're Jews.*

One other thought about Jews and money. I think that one reason why antisemitism is sometimes not recognized as such is because people contort that association in order to imagine that it isn't negative. In 2014, three people from the world of soccer reiterated the idea that Jews are rich. Malky Mackay, the then Cardiff City manager, was discovered to have sent a text saying, "Nothing like a Jew that sees money slipping through his fingers." Dave Whelan, the Wigan Athletic owner, said: "Jewish people chase money more than everybody else." And the forward Mario Balotelli, while at Manchester City, reposted a tweet in which Super Mario is compared to a Jew because he's good at grabbing coins.

When it was pointed out to these men that, possibly, there was something problematic about these comments, all three couldn't quite grasp why. Whelan, in fact, tried to suggest his was a compliment, by saying that Jews are "shrewd people." This is telling. It tells us two things. First, that Whelan thinks that it's not an insult to link Jews with money, because money's a good thing, isn't it? In a capitalist society, we admire people with money. Except of course, we don't. We envy and resent people with money. And we particularly envy and resent people with money around whom we can create narratives, racist narratives, that suggest that there is something dark, ill-gotten, and exploitative about how they, and all their brethren they are in league with, got that money. Second, it tells us that most tropes about Jews being rich aren't just about them being rich. The word "shrewd" implies something else. As with Mackay's and Balotelli's stereo-types, these aren't fantasies of richness, but of miserli-ness: of a pinched, obsessive, inhuman ability to run, leap, grab, and keep money.

I am, I would say, one of the U.K.'s very few famous Jews. By which I don't mean I am one of the U.K.'s very few famous—ish—people who are Jewish. There's quite a number of those. What I mean is that I am one of the very few people in this country whose Jewishness is one of the principal things known about them. Who else is there? The actress Dame Maureen Lipman, possibly. Television and radio presenter Vanessa Feltz. Some media rabbis. That's kind of it. Within British comedy there are many other Jews (or, at least, people with Jewish heritage)—Matt Lucas, Stephen Fry, Alexei Sayle, Simon Amstell, Sue Perkins, Simon Brodkin, Robert Popper, Ben Elton*—but I'd say that only I am someone who most people would know, if they know me at all, as Jewish. Only I, that is, have made being Jewish part of my public identity.

I think this absence is partly because—until very recently—being British and Jewish wasn't really a thing. Jews may be the only minority group in this country who have never been cool. (Unlike their American counterparts—think Mort Sahl or Saul Bellow in 1963—cool as fuck.†)

---

* Not a point really in the remit of this book, but it is indicative of the dominance of American popular culture that if this was a list of U.S. comedians, a British reader would probably know them all. I'm assuming you know very few of them, so you'll have to trust me, they are all well known in the U.K., and all very funny.

† This is partly because American Jews are American, and British Jews are British. Which means the American ones are loud and confident, whereas the British ones are reserved and polite (generalizations: I *know*). Someone once said to me that the headline of the *Jewish Chronicle* (founded in 1841 in London, and the oldest continuously published Jewish newspaper in the world), every week, is "They Hate Us." I said, no, it's "They Hate Us: And Let's Not Make a Fuss About It." British Jewishness has, for years, smacked of suburbia. Of Stanmore (a very suburban—and fairly Jewish populated—suburb of London). The idea that Jewish, as an ethnicity, as an identity, can be cool, in the way that most others can be, still seems a bit absurd.

But beyond not being cool, there is also, around Jews, and their Jewishness, some shame. Here is a conversation I had with a woman at a wedding once:

> WOMAN: Oh you're David Baddiel. You're Jewish, aren't you?
>
> ME: Yes.
>
> WOMAN: I'm Jewish. Although you probably can't tell, can you? That'll be the nose job.
>
> ME: Right ...
>
> WOMAN: I never normally tell people. That I'm Jewish, I mean.
>
> ME: Why not?
>
> WOMAN: (*as if it's obvious*) Well. People don't like 'em.

Amazing though this wedding guest's attitude was—her breezy acceptance of Jew-hate, and also, of something even deeper, the acceptance of a default distinction between Jews and People—I don't think it was that unusual. The actress Miriam Margolyes,* in an interview in the U.K.'s *Daily Telegraph* in 2015, said: "Look, nobody likes Jews. You can't say people like Jews. We're not popular. We're too smart to be liked." Margolyes is different from the wedding guest in that she is outspokenly

---

* I hate doing this to Miriam, who has had an amazing and varied career but: Professor Sprout from the *Harry Potter* films.

progressive and of the left, and, like many left-wing Jews, carries particular shame around Israel, but her statement feels deeper than that, more universal and eternal (she preceded it by saying that "the English are naturally anti-semitic'). It also has another very Jewish wrinkle in it, which is Jews' own reflection back to mainstream culture of the high-low status duality projected on to them: we are hated because we are smart.

Significantly, one of the things that marks Jewishness out as different from other ethnicities is that it *can* be hidden. One of the many contradictory beliefs held by antisemites is that Jews are incredibly, obviously Jewish—because they all have big noses and swarthy skin and dark hair and are fattened up with their own greed—and simultaneously diffi-cult to spot, which is what allows them to get under the radar of non-Jews and work their despicable secret doings. This is why the Nazis were able to have cartoons of Jews that depicted them in a very recognizable, uniformly grotesque manner—big noses, swarthy skin, dark hair, fattened with their own greed—but also extensive and complex checks for spotting Jews. And, of course, the requirement of Jews to wear armbands that identified them as Jews.

This ability to hide is important in the omission of Jews from identity politics, because most identities, sexual ones aside, are fairly impossible to hide. Jews can hide; they can pass as non-Jews. So the assumption appears to be that because they are not immediately visible, they don't suffer racism. Jews don't really suffer from being considered different, because they don't *look* different. But consider what the woman at the wedding said. She doesn't tell people she's Jewish, because "people don't like them." Which would suggest that Jews don't really suffer from being thought of as different as long as people don't know they're Jews: as long as they, like gays in the closet, hide. Which means that Jews are only OK as long as they can pass as non-Jews, and that Jews—once identified as such—*will* be thought of as different.

I'm not someone given to hiding my Jewishness.* My Twitter biography has always been one word: Jew.

David Baddiel ✔
@Baddiel

Jew

⊙ London   🔗 davidbaddiel.com   📅 Joined January 2009

2,328 Following   **721.3K** Followers

---

* Those who have followed my stand-up and TV work will be aware that I'm not given to hiding anything. I tend to be absurdly, wearily, open about everything about my life. I have monetized being myself as a career.

This is for a number of reasons, none of them to do with religion. First, it's funny. Second, it's a statement against Jewish shame, and indeed Jewish absence, against Jews not counting, by putting it—however comically—front and center of my identity. And number three, it's a reclamation, although a twisted one. "Jew" has a strange status, as a bad word. All other minorities, in the process of reclaiming hate speech, are working with words that aren't actually the words in the dictionary that describe them. They are reclaiming slang insults. Jew *is* actually what I am. So it's interesting that those concerned about offense tend to say "Jewish people" rather than "Jew." Because even though it is the correct word, and not a slang word coined by racists, the deep burial of it in a bad place in the Christian unconscious means that it feels insulting *anyway*. The avoidance of the word brings home, in fact, the—to coin a phrase—systemic racism of Judeo-Christian culture, the submerged power that hangs around, because of two centuries of linguistic toxicity. In my novel, *The Secret Purposes*, which is about the internment of German Jewish refugees on the Isle of Man during World War Two—something that happened to my grandfather, and a part of British history so little known that by itself it figures, I would suggest, as an example of Jewish absence from the culture—a translator called June is working on the transcript of an interview she's conducted with a character called Frau Spitzy, one of the few genuine Nazis sharing the island with the Jews, and this happens:

A: I would much rather share my quarters with Aryan men than Jewish women.

June picked up her pen, poising it above the words "Jewish women". They weren't quite right. Frau Spitzy's exact sentence was *Ich werde viel lieber meine Viertel mit Aryan Mann als Judinnen teilt*. *Judinnen*: not "Judische Frauen", which in June's linguistically correct heart she knew was the actual correspondence with "Jewish women". *Judinnen*: it was simply the feminine plural of *Jude*, Jew, female Jews ... Jewesses? No, didn't quite cut it in English— too biblical. And then there was Frau Spitzy's tone, effortlessly, reflexively contemptuous—suddenly, she saw it. With her pen, June scrubbed out the three letters, i, s, h, the suffix, so the sentence read:

A: I would much rather share my quarters with Aryan men than Jew women.

That was it. A miniscule change—just one stroke of the pen—but it made all the difference. Suddenly, June had successfully conveyed the insulting spirit of the Nazi woman's words. At first, she felt guiltily pleased with herself, but then realised with a start that this would always be the case with *Jew* as opposed to *Jewish*. A Jewish lawyer—a Jew lawyer. A Jewish banker—a Jew banker. A Jewish boy—a Jew boy. The words ran in her mind, changing from white to black as she said them. Racking her vocabulary-rich brain, June could not think of another word that you could do this with, where you could use the noun as an adjective in this manner. Why did dropping the suffix have such an effect? Was it that it implied that the speaker had so little time for Jews he would not even spare them the consideration of grammar? Or perhaps ... saying a man is a Jewish banker implies that the man is a banker who happens to be a Jew, but saying that the same man is a Jew banker implies that he is primarily and always will be a Jew, whatever his job—the word itself will not change because he and all the others that share his race will never change. And beyond her intellectualisations and rationalisations, June realised, as she had not before, that the word itself, *Jew*, that is, not Jewish, or Judaic, but the word stripped bare, *Jude*, carried with it a streaming virulent energy: that within its tiny syllable was contained all the time and all the fear and all the hate of its history. This is what makes the gentile want to spit it out of his mouth.

I have never tried to hide my Jewishness, except on one occasion, involving *The Secret Purposes*. I went into my local branch of UK bookstore chain Waterstones soon after the book came out in 2004, and saw that it had been placed in something called the Jewish Interest section. I felt a very strong urge to take it out of there and place it somewhere else in the store.

And not just the Highly Recommended section. In interviews before *The Secret Purposes* came out, I talked about how it was principally a love story, and as much about British history as about Jewishness. This was because I didn't want it to be bought and read only by Jews. So it was a bit depressing that on the Amazon site for *The Secret Purposes*, under the section People Who Bought This Book Also Bought, you'd find Amos Oz this, Anita Brookner that, various books with Hitler in the title, and *How to Raise a Jewish Dog* by The Rabbis of the Boca Raton Theological Seminary.

However, I don't really think this was about trying to hide my Jewishness. I think it was, in truth, the opposite. I was reacting to the creation, in that bookstore, of a ghetto. There was no Asian or Black Interest Section in that Waterstones. Because that would be to mark out those ethnicities, and authors from those ethnicities, as separate from the culture at large. While there would be a high awareness that the authors of books such as *White Teeth* or *Brick Lane*—Zadie Smith and Monica Ali respectively—

were people of color, and that be a positive thing, there would be no sense, in a bookstore, that these works should occupy a somehow separate-from-the-rest-of-modern-British-fiction category. The opposite in fact: such novels were/are hailed—correctly—as prime examples of great new British writing, products of a diversity simply representative of how Britain is now.

I cannot think of a British Jewish novel where this is the case (in America, again, it's different, from Saul Bellow and Philip Roth to Jonathan Safran Foer and Nicole Krauss). The most famous Jewish novelist in Britain is Howard Jacobson who won the Man Booker Prize for *The Finkler Question* in 2010. But, although he has won the Booker, his works are still seen fundamentally as Jewish novels, and not expressive, in social terms, of anything beyond that ethnicity. If you want to find a book that *is* considered entirely metonymic of the country now, look no further than the 2019 Booker Prize winner, Bernardine Evaristo's *Girl, Woman, Other*, of which the *New Statesman* said, "If you want to understand modern day Britain, this is the writer to read." You will not find a blurb like that on the back of *The Finkler Question*, or any other British novel whose Jewishness is on the front foot.

The problem is that Jews occupy a socio-cultural gray area. Jews, although marginal, are not thought of as *marginalized*. Which means Jews can't be seen as representative of a modern Britain that is intent on shifting marginalized experiences into the mainstream. Jews, therefore, as far as progressives are concerned, don't *represent* anything outside of themselves. No victory is claimed by championing their experience, and this leads to a subtle—and unconscious—exclusion.

Sometimes the unconscious attitudes of progressives toward Jews come out in weird ways, such as when the then leader of the Labour Party, Jeremy Corbyn, pronounced, on a TV debate, the name of the pedophile, sex-trafficker Jeffrey Epstein as "Epshteen." This was taken, by some, as unconsciously highlighting the Jewishness of a very unsavory character. I have no idea, not being Jeremy's shrink, whether antisemitism was in his subconscious here or not, but when I said, on Twitter,* "Every Jew noticed that"—a truism—I was massively shouted at by Corbyn's followers.

It's the shouting, rather than Corbyn's pronunciation itself, that demonstrates the unconscious attitudes. Those people shouting at me would be the same people who would shout at Piers Morgan if he, say, claimed that there is nothing racist about the treatment of Meghan

---

* There's going to be a fair few references in this book to Twitter. I apologize to any readers not on it. But, for better or worse, the truth is that most of the cultural conversation about identity politics takes place on social media these days, and probably foremost on that platform.

Markle in the British press. The same people would immediately point out that Morgan cannot speak about racism against people of color, having never suffered it—it is the prerogative of those on the receiving end of any specific racism to define that racism. *They* get to say what is and isn't racist, and Piers Morgan does not.

Someone who wasn't shouting at me was Laura Murray, the head of complaints at the Labour Party, who wrote a very polite email to me following this tweet, saying that she hoped I didn't really think that Corbyn's pronunciation of Epstein as Epshteen had any meaning, subconscious or otherwise. Which is not what I said. I said, "Every Jew noticed that." We live in a culture now where impact is more important than intent; where how things are taken is more significant than how they are meant. You have to listen to the people being talked about rather than the talker—and the power, throughout history, has tended to be with the talker, the person with the platform, rather than the talked-about, who are usually the ones affected.

I do not know whether or not this is a good thing. But it is a thing. It exists: our discourse has shifted in favor of the talked-about. It is a progressive article of faith—much heightened during the Black Lives Matter protests following the murder of George Floyd in 2020—that those who do not experience racism need to listen, to learn, to accept and not challenge, when others speak about their

JEWS DON'T COUNT

experiences. Except, it seems, when Jews do. Non-Jews, including progressive non-Jews, are still very happy to tell Jews whether or not the utterance about them was in fact racist.

This is partly because anti-Jewish racism is not, in many people's minds, racism at all. It has, after all, a different name, and one hears talk all the time of "antisemitism and racism." That has value, in some ways, because not all racisms *are* the same. Racism against people of color *is* different in kind to racism against Jews. The question in this book is why a difference in kind should equate to a difference in significance.

Unfortunately, the separation of antisemitism from racism also creates for some a sense that it is a different thing entirely. When online I talk about racism against Jews, people—from both left and right—sometimes decide to object by saying that Jews are not a race and therefore cannot suffer racism. This is an old canard, generally employed by those who have learned that racism is bad, but can't be doing with extending that sufferance to Jews: and so they downgrade the category of antisemitism to that of religious intolerance. Which gives them more of a free hand with Jews, as religious intolerance is *not as bad* as racism. (In fact, religious intolerance could almost be seen as a good thing in this view, religion being a belief system with power and money attached, worthy of satire and mockery.)

Except antisemitism has very little to do with religion. As I have often said, I'm an atheist and yet the Gestapo would shoot me tomorrow.* Racists who don't like Jews never ask the Jew they are abusing how often they go to synagogue. They just see the Jewish name and they know. Which is why it's racism. One's Jewishness, just like one's skin color, is an accident of birth, and as far as the racists are concerned—and they, sadly, are the people that matter as far as racism goes—you can never lose either.

When my progressive friend says "But the Y-word isn't as bad as the N-word?" however stunned I might be, at some level I'm not. At some level, actually, I'm grateful to him for laying out the discrepancy in attitude toward different racisms so clearly. And that thought is: Yes, all right, anti-semitism isn't nice but let's not compare it to racism against Black and Brown people. Jews are, after all, white. Aren't they?

Many progressives would say they are. Mear One—real name Kalen Ockerman—is the street artist who painted the mural that was at the center of one particular chapter

---

* I'm not entirely sure why I say tomorrow, as they would no doubt shoot me today, but tomorrow sounds more appropriate. This may be from watching too many films where Nazis find Jews in hiding and then take them somewhere to be shot.

in the book, *He's an Anti-Semite vs No He Isn't, It's a Disgusting Smear*: the book, in other words, of the former Labour Party leader Jeremy Corbyn. This mural, which was painted on a wall in east London, and depicted a troupe of capitalist bankers playing Monopoly on the backs of the world's poor, was taken down by the council in 2012 after complaints from local Jews. Mear One, of course, is a *total* progressive. He couldn't be more woke.* I mean: he's a street artist.

And yet, his mural was racist. Or, at least, Jews seemed to think so. How could this be? To put it stupidly, how could someone so apparently left-wing be accused of something so apparently right-wing?

Mear One's own reaction to the buffing of his mural was instructive. He said: "Some of the older white Jewish folk in the local community had a problem with me portraying their beloved #Rothschild or #Warburg." Ignore the patronizing, Goebbels-like, insinuating tone— one that would never be used by anyone "woke" toward any other ethnic minority—and instead consider why Mear decided to add hashtags to those names.

---

* I've been avoiding this word so far. It might have been easier to use it earlier—as shorthand for the progressives on the right side of history, etc.—but I think it's become an overused, somewhat lazy word recently, particularly in its use as a scratching post for free speech warriors. Plus the word originated in the civil rights movement, and I respect that usage. However, it does, I think, describe how Mear One would see himself.

It was posted on his Facebook page, and thus these hashtagged names can be clicked on. This means that Mear is not just saying: "I have painted Rothschild, the Jewish banking scion," but: "I have painted Rothschild, the Jewish banking scion whose name you can now follow into the darkest corners of the internet, which will help you understand how this Jewish banking scion controls the world."

But I think more important is Mear's deliberate addition of the word "white." As we know, almost any attack on the status quo these days comes with the assumption that the enemy is white and straight and a man, but white is the high point of the trilogy. I agree with that. I agree that being white can bring with it enormous privilege, a lot of which the white person isn't even aware of.

But Jews are not white. Or not quite.* Or, at least, they don't always feel it. I'm not referring here to the fact that some Jews perceived as Caucasian are of Middle Eastern

---

* It's worth saying early on in this book that some of this may not speak to Jews of color. I accept this, and indeed, apologize for it. My argument rests on how progressives view Jews in contrast to how they view other minorities, and Jews of color—indeed, any Jew who is also a member of another minority—may not experience this discrepancy in exactly the same way. I particularly accept that my point about the not-quite-whiteness of Jews in general may have no resonance for those Jews who are clearly non-white. And who sometimes, for that very reason, have to suffer discrimination against them from other Jews. There is another book to be written—not by me—about that experience.

descent, and their melanin can follow suit. One of my first jokes on starting stand-up was: "I've been beaten up twice in my life, once for being Jewish, one for being a Pakistani." I mean that being white is not about skin color, but security. It means you are protected because you are a member of the majority culture. Protected, that is, from prejudice, discrimination, second-class citizenship, dispossession, and genocide. Which Jews—as, perhaps, you've guessed I was about to say—have not always been. So what Mear was doing by ignoring that historical truth about Jews—by calling them "white'— was reinforcing his credentials as Fighter for the Oppressed. He's saying: Yes, I'm caricaturing Jews, but that's OK because they are Privilege, and Power, and Control, and all the other things contained in the word "white." Jews are The Man, and my job as a Street Artist is Sticking It To The Man.

That's where Jeremy Corbyn comes in. Here's Jeremy, in 2012, with not even a sniff of his oncoming destiny yet: Jeremy sees the Street Artist being taken down and Jeremy's rebel radar is up. He spots, of course, the old Marxist, historical parallels involving the names Lenin and Rockefeller and Diego Rivera, and he weighs in behind Mear on Facebook.

What he doesn't spot is the antisemitism. He doesn't notice the other historical parallels you might have thought were blindingly obvious: between the mural and the depictions of hook-nosed Jewish bankers holding the world to ransom that were published every week in the Nazi newspaper *Der Stürmer*. He doesn't see that the mural could be a cover of almost any reprint of *The Protocols of the Elders of Zion*, the fake text from 1903 that purports to reveal a Jewish plot for world domination.

That's not because Corbyn is necessarily, in the active sense to which I referred earlier, an antisemite. He is, like Mear One, a rebel, a champion of the oppressed. There is a video of Corbyn speaking emotionally at a demonstration to remember the 1936 Battle of Cable Street, in which Oswald Mosley's fascists were driven back from their march in the East End of London. The Jews in this situation, onto whose houses Mosley's blackshirts daubed the Y-word, were clearly oppressed. Jeremy Corbyn can speak passionately for them, his voice breaking. But present-day, middle-income Jews, upset and frightened by the grotesque depiction of what seems to them to be Jews on the walls of that same East End that Mosley marched through—not so much.

I'm not sure, however, that Corbyn even knew the mural was meant to depict Rothschild and Warburg. He won't have seen that. Because he will have seen something else first: a gesture against capitalist power. This is the key to the charge of antisemitism around Corbyn. Corbyn is not someone who hates Jews but someone—like most progressives, like my friend who contended that the Y-word was not as bad as the N-word—who places anti-Jewish racism lower on the hierarchy of things that truly matter. So low, in fact, that it might not even feature. A later example of this would be Corbyn's pre-election TV interview with Andrew Neil on BBC 1 in 2019. In it Neil read out a quote from a Labour Party Facebook group that included the words "Rothschild bankers control Israel and world governments" and then asked Corbyn if that was something he would consider antisemitic. It is, of course, a standard example of high-status racism: the idea of Jews controlling the world through secrecy and finance. Corbyn would not say it was antisemitic. It took him a number of answers and evasions (and this at a time when it would be politic to just condemn such a statement out of hand) before he finally said it might be considered an antisemitic trope. And here's the point. Someone like Corbyn will see the anticapitalism in that sentence before the antisemitism. He *can* be brought to see the antisemitism, grudgingly, but another part of him would always be deeply resistant to having to shut down or condemn an anticapitalist statement at all. Anticapitalism is at his core. When it is pointed out to him that sometimes anticapitalism blurs into antisemitism, his first instinct is to protect the anticapitalism and dismiss the antisemitism with irritation.

It would not be fair, I think, to suggest that Corbyn noticed the potential antisemitism of the images in that mural and *then* dismissed it as irrelevant. It wouldn't even have been in the frame.

His frame, that is: *his* vision of the mural. However, antisemitism very much *is* in the mural's frame. There is, on both left and right, a very long history of capitalist power being represented as Jewish power. This developed out of an esthetic that is far older than capitalism itself, one in which, since at least the late thirteenth century, Jews were routinely painted and sculpted as gargoyles and devils. Our artistic tradition—look at Punch and Judy, look at witches, look at pantomime, look at Bond villains—depicts evil as swarthy and hook-nosed. We have, in our deepest collective unconsciousness, the face of Satan—whoever our Satan may be—as the face of the Jew. The left, for all its antiracist credentials, has never balked at that—the Jew face, the Jew hair, the Jew fat banker smoking his fat cigar—imagery. It remains the primary way in which to portray the scheming, evil, capitalist enemy. And if you can't see a problem with this—if you just think, Well, that's how our enemy looks—you are accepting it. It's a default.

I have talked before about Jews not being white, online—and indeed used the hashtag #Jewsnotwhite—and each time I notice some progressives bristle at the idea. I acknowledge, of course, that Jews can "pass" as non-Jews, and therefore can, except in historical cases, when their ethnicity has been forcibly outed by the legal imposition on their clothing of yellow stars or other insignia, avoid the kind of immediate, on-sight racism that people of color daily suffer from. But still: antiracists need to listen more to the enemy. Because antiracism only exists to fight racists; it only has meaning oppositionally. If there were no racists, there would be no antiracists. And the racists say: Jews are not white. The Nazis said it all the time—the project of the Jews, as far as they were concerned, was to undermine the Aryan white races. And the exclusion of Jews from the category of whiteness is still key to present-day white supremacists. Here is Article V of Harold Covington's Constitution for the Ethno-State, a bible for American white nationalists: "The race commonly known as Jews are in culture and historic tradition an Asiatic people, and shall not be considered White or accorded White racial status under law."

In fact, this exclusion of Jews from whiteness is funda-mental to the ideology of white supremacists. The Charlottesville riots of 2017 were precipitated by a rally called Unite the Right. Something many people noticed was that the main chant the torch-holding, white, foot soldiers were marching to was: "The Jews will not replace us!" At first, this seemed confusing. I posted on Twitter:

David Baddiel ✔
@Baddiel

Well obviously not. The tiki lamps, the shirt, the dumb self-serious expression: we couldn't do any of it.

Jews will not replace us!

But I'd misunderstood. The chant—which was initially posted by Richard Spencer, the prominent neo-Nazi who led the protest, as an instruction—is an expression of a conspiracy theory, called the Great Replacement, which states that Jews are secretly masterminding the promotion of immigration and multiculturalism in order to undermine, and eventually replace, Aryan whites. Jews are not trying to replace whites with Jews. They are trying to replace whites with Browns and Blacks, and pulling the strings to do so. This conspiracy theory has deep roots in the far right. It is the reason why eleven Jews were murdered in Pittsburgh in 2018. Before his actions, the killer, Robert Bowers, posted on the ultra-right-wing social media site Gab that the Hebrew Immigrant Aid Society (a charity associated with the Tree of Life synagogue, which raised money for refugees) was, in his words, bringing "invaders in that kill our people."

To understand this, you need to reconsider what I said earlier about Jews being the only objects of racism to whom a double status is applied, both high and low. In the Great Replacement, Jews are not white—they can't be, as they are operating against the white races and they are the whites' main enemy—but they are not Brown or Black either, because they are utilizing those races for their secret, world-conquering purposes. Jews, for the racists, don't have a skin color. That's part of their dastardly power. Jews are invisible, working their terrible magic behind the global scenes, and they don't even have a visual mark. Unless, of course, you're one of those specific racists with the superpower to spot that underneath, Jews are lizards.

Either way, racists say Jews aren't white. Problem is, progressives, in general, tend to think they are white and, therefore, not really deserving of the protections progressive movements offer to non-white people facing racism. In some cases, Jews and Jewishness are used to signify even greater whiteness than normal. Jessica Krug is very much a progressive: her online biography described her as an associate professor at George Washington University, who has written extensively about Africa, Latin America, the diaspora, and identity, while claiming her own Black and Latina heritage. But in September 2020, she came out as white. Like the more well-known Rachel Dolezal before her, she had been living a lie. Unlike Rachel Dolezal however, much of the reporting around Krug didn't just say that she was white: she was described, frequently, as "white and Jewish."

> ## 'Black' professor Jessica Krug admits that she is really white and Jewish

Why? How is Jewishness relevant? Well, according to the law of Schrödinger's Whites, a brilliant conceit that I am not responsible for, in which Jews are white or non-white depending on the politics of the observer, in this context Krug's Jewishness enhances the story. She's not Black. That's the story. And one way of making this into even more of a story, to make her opposition to what she pretended to be even *more* pointed, is to play up her Jewishness, as if Jewishness somehow adds extra white-ness to her whiteness. Buried deeply inside here is a double racism: an idea that Jews are rich, something Black people are assumed not to be, and that therefore the implication of struggle and difficulty, of victim status, that Krug was hoping to associate with herself, has been *particularly* wiped out because she is Jewish. Because Jews do not have struggle and difficulty, Jews cannot be victims. Despite what two thousand years of history tells us.

As I don't like to leave out complexity, I will add that Krug herself, in the blog where she came out, said: "I have eschewed my lived experience as a white Jewish child in suburban Kansas City." Apart from the fact that mentioning her own Jewishness is not a reason for it to be continually highlighted in the press, it's clear to anyone reading that blog that Jessica Krug, like other Jews I've talked about, is deeply self-loathing. That Jessica Krug hates herself for being white and Jewish, and completely buys into the myth that Jewishness represents privilege and power, and so, while covering herself in the sackcloth and ashes fitting to someone finally telling the truth about such a lie—particularly such an offensive lie—it's important for her to own that privilege and power. It's important for her, in other words, to accord with the story.

Consider the acronym BAME. Criticized often, but none-theless extremely present as a usage in the current conversation around race in the U.K., it has a distinct difference from the parallel U.S. BIPOC: it stands for

Black, Asian, and Minority Ethnic. Jews are an ethnic minority. But in Britain, recently, Sajid Javid was hailed as the first BAME Chancellor of the Exchequer, despite the fact that Margaret Thatcher's Chancellor Nigel Lawson was and is Jewish. In 2017, progressives were angry because the BBC published a list of its highest-paid broadcasters, and none of them was from a BAME background—despite that list including Claudia Winkleman and Vanessa Feltz. I myself wrote to Mohit Bakaya, after he was announced as the first BAME head of BBC Radio 4, to congratulate him and point out that the Jewish Mark Damazer actually got there before him, but no one noticed (Mohit said it made him laugh).

But perhaps we can cut to the chase on this. Let me ask you, dear reader, a straight question: do you think of Jews as BAME? I mean, I do, but that's partly the point of this book: it's a polemic, about why Jews *should* be understood as somewhere in the ME section of BAME. But I think most people would not agree. They might decide to not actively exclude Jews, once someone like me points out to them that Jews are actually an ethnic minority, who get discriminated against and suffer racism. But that acceptance would be accompanied, I would suggest, by a kind of *oh yeah, I suppose so, never really thought about it like that* shrug.

BAME carries with it an image, which is dependent on skin color. It also carries with it, hopefully—although obviously this often fails in practice—a benefit. If you're

BAME you should—that's what the category is there for—benefit from positive discrimination. Jews don't. Jews are an ethnic minority, and they simply don't. Google it. Try and find any example of Jews in business, in education, in politics, in cultural institutions, being given a leg-up as a result of their ethnicity. That's because they don't need it, I feel you thinking. But what does that mean, and where does that thought lead?

To take my own business, that of show. No indie film producer intent on inclusivity has ever thought, OK, we're keen to cast more Jewish actors in this movie; no interesting avant-garde theater director has ever said, "I want to make sure that there's diversity in this cast, get Maureen Lipman's agent on the phone." I myself have been in meetings about TV shows and heard people say—correctly—we need to make sure this show is genuinely diverse, and it crosses my mind to say, well, I'm Jewish, but I never do because I know it will just be met with a blank look. Like: *yeah, so?*

As regards the controversial area of minority casting, Jew remains the only minority—and now we're talking beyond ethnic, to include disabled, trans, autistic, and many other categories—where you don't have to cast the actor in line with the real thing. There will be instant outrage, and consequences, to the casting of, say, a trans part to anyone but a trans actor: *Rub & Tug*, a 2018 movie about a trans sex-worker, which was due to star cis actress

Scarlett Johansson, was halted after protests from the trans community, and similarly, Halle Berry was briefly canceled—let's not go into what that means—in 2020 after announcing that she was looking forward to researching what would be required to play a trans man in another film. A trans part must go to a trans actor, a disabled part to a disabled actor, and so on.*

Meanwhile, in the 2019 TV drama *McMafia*, James Norton (educated at Ampleforth, a Roman Catholic boarding school) played the main part, a Jew, Alex Godman. In *Disobedience*, a film about a lesbian couple in an orthodox London community, one of the leads, Rachel Weisz, is Jewish but the other two main actors, Rachel McAdams and Alessandro Nivola, are not. Just one of the four family members portrayed in the only long-running sitcom on British TV that could claim to be ostensibly Jewish,

---

* A caveat here. I noticed that when the film *Supernova* came out in 2020, there was no outrage. It's a love story between two gay men starring the straight actors Stanley Tucci and Colin Firth. In fact it was reviewed extremely positively. There was still a conversation about it, and Firth spoke of his uncertainty about taking the role, saying "I don't have a final position about this. I think the question is still alive." Which is not a discussion that happens much with non-Jews playing Jews. But I also think that there is a specific issue of bravery around the idea of playing a gay man on screen. Because for years in the cinema, to do so would have been considered damaging to a career (and obviously, also for years, actors who were gay would pretend to be straight). It is still, I would suggest, considered in some way brave for a major straight actor to play a gay man in a mainstream movie. It is not brave for a non-Jew to play a Jew.

Channel 4's *Friday Night Dinner*, Tom Rosenthal, is actually Jewish, and he has renounced that heritage in interviews.* The examples are too numerous to list, but here's a scoop for you I discovered while writing this book. The British actress Sarah Solemani, who is Jewish, told me she screen-tested for the lead role in *The Marvelous Mrs. Maisel*. She said, in fact, that the final decision was between her and Rachel Brosnahan, who is not Jewish. Brosnahan got the part. Here's the thing about *The Marvelous Mrs. Maisel*. It's about comedy, but really it's about Jews. It's about as Jewish as a TV show can be. Rachel Brosnahan is very good in the main part, but—my Jewdar is acute—I knew instantly that she wasn't Jewish. And I don't really have a problem with that. Or I wouldn't, were I not aware that every single other minority, in a show where the way of being of that minority was central, would have needed to be cast accordingly. The producers would simply not have countenanced the reaction otherwise.

---

* He said in a *Guardian* interview, "The last proper Jew in our family was four generations back." Interestingly, I was once interviewed by his dad, TV soccer presenter Jim Rosenthal. It was on a big match day, a Saturday, outside Wembley Stadium. I said, jokingly, "Should you really be here on Shabbos, Jim?" Jim stopped the interview, and very pressingly made the point that he wasn't Jewish. "I get out of that because of my dad," he said. Which is weird, as most Jews, who worry about that kind of stuff, prescribe Jewishness as coming down the mother's line. Either way, it's not up to me to tell Jim Rosenthal he is Jewish (I actually bumped into him much later on in a sauna, naked, and it still seemed to me he was, but anyway).

Similarly, in *Hunters*, a show about Nazi hunting on Amazon, Al Pacino plays the main part, Meyer Offerman.* Al Pacino I think we know is Italian-American, and not Jewish. When it came out in 2020, the film *Mank*, about the *Citizen Kane* screenwriter Herman Mankiewicz, got amazing reviews. Mankiewicz was Jewish, and it's not shied from in the film: he talks in various scenes of the *ganze mispocha*, which is Yiddish for the whole family. The part is played by the non-Jewish Gary Oldman. Oldman isn't just not Jewish, however. In a 2014 *Playboy* interview, Oldman defended Mel Gibson and his infamous antisemitic rant when arrested in 2006 by saying that those offended should "get over it." He added: "Mel Gibson is in a town that's run by Jews and he said the wrong thing because he's actually bitten the hand that I guess has fed him, and doesn't need to feed him anymore because he's got enough dough."

Oldman later apologized, in a very fulsome and thought-out manner. But still: there hasn't been a murmur about this. Not a murmur about the fact that perpetuating the myth of the Jewish stranglehold over Hollywood might be an issue for casting him as a Jewish screenwriter, in a film which represents, sometimes pretty negatively, a lot of other Jewish players in Hollywood at the time. Again, I'm not saying Oldman

---

* But see footnote, page 65.

should not have been given this part; nor am I calling for any retraction of awards for his performance (although he does mispronounce *mispocha*). I'm saying there should be, as there would have been with any other minority, a conversation about it.*

Meanwhile, in HBO's *The Plot Against America*, a rabbi is played by John Turturro. Interestingly, he was questioned about this, although not in any way aggressively and not with any sense that it might be a problem. He said: "I feel like an honorary Jew. My wife is Jewish, my kids are Jewish. I mean I grew up in New York City, so I'm basically Jewish!" Well, good for you, John, although a) I'd like to have seen what would have happened had Halle Berry tried to breeze through the accusations of transphobia in a similarly amiable manner, and b) the joke about New York is a racist one, not a million miles from calling it Hymietown. As I've said, it's not active antisemitism that I'm banging on about here, it's passive. Look for the absence: the absence, in this case, of concern. What is John Turturro *not* doing here? He's not concerned about microaggressions to Jews. Because there is not a proper call-out culture around those.

---

* I am fairly sure, for example, that even though, as I mentioned in an earlier footnote, it is acceptable for straight actors to play gay roles, it would not be acceptable—certainly not without a conversation—for a straight actor who had publicly made homophobic comments.

However, if he was cast as a gay character in a TV drama, I think he'd think very carefully, with a lot of concern about the consequences, before saying "I mean I grew up in San Francisco, so I'm basically gay." If we lived in a time when any actor could play any part, I would not be calling for non-Jewish actors to be barred from playing Jewish parts. Indeed, I'm not calling for it now. I'm pointing out the discrepancy, the fact that there is no outrage. Certainly not on the scale of *Rub & Tug*, where Johansson pulled out and the entire movie was scrapped.*

---

* One particular area where there is avid monitoring of the rights and wrongs of ethnic casting is animation. I'm a huge fan of the Netflix animation show *BoJack Horseman*. It's a stone-cold masterpiece, in my opinion the best comedy drama on TV of the last decade (not the best animated one, the best one). An issue that has dogged this show, however, and that the creator Raphael Bob-Waksberg has spent a lot of time apologizing for, is that one of the main female characters, Diane Nguyen, is American-Vietnamese, but is voiced by the white American actress Alison Brie. Recently, Waksberg posted a very long Twitter thread in which he explained at great length how that—as he put it—error was made, and how much he has learned since and the amends the show has made for it. He did this because no doubt he feels bad about it, but also because there was, within the world of animation fans, a very large outcry about the casting of Diane. Meanwhile, the character of Lenny Turtletaub, who is Jewish—a very Jewish Hollywood producer stereotype, funny, but a stereotype—is played by J.K. Simmons, who is not Jewish. There has been no outcry about that, and Waksberg has seen no need to get anguished about it.

While we're on the subject, I noticed something about *BoJack*, as it went on: it's a show in which characters can be human or animal. Most varieties of animals turn up in its six seasons. But I spotted an absence in it, which at first I thought odd, as they are arguably the

There is never any real outrage about non-Jews playing Jews; although there was an attempt recently in a column in the *Jewish Chronicle*. In September 2019, a musical called *Falsettos*, previously on Broadway, opened in London. As far as I can make out—I haven't seen it— *Falsettos* is pretty Jewish; all the characters are Jewish and the first song is called "Four Jews in a Room, Bitching." When it opened in London, none of the cast was Jewish. The outrage went as far as a letter to *The Stage*, in which a new word was coined: Jewface. The letter was signed by various Jewish actors, writers and directors, and reiterated some of the most recent examples of Jewish parts being played by non-Jewish actors:

most humanoid animals: there are no apes or monkeys in *BoJack Horseman*. Cats, bulls, deer, horses, of course, turtles, as in Lenny Turtletaub, manatees, but no primates. Then I worked out why: I think that, considering that each animal essentially stands in for a human type (BoJack, a horse, is a washed-up sex-and-drug addict nineties sitcom star), there might be an anxiety in the writers' room of the horrific possibility of viewers *mistaking* monkey or ape characters for corresponding humans of color. So much so that they decided to just miss out that class of animals. Until the last episode of the entire series, in which a character called Danny Bananas appears. Danny is voiced by Phil Rosenthal, the Jewish producer of *Everybody Loves Raymond*, and is clearly a Jewish character. It's good that a Jewish character is played by a Jewish actor. However, Danny Bananas *is* a monkey: a proboscis monkey.

Where were the protests over Jewface when non-Jewish performers played the following Jewish roles, to name but a few: James McArdle as Louis (*Angels in America*, National Theatre), Simon Russell Beale as Chaim Lehman (*The Lehman Trilogy*, NT), Lauren Ward as Rose Stopnick Gellman (*Caroline, or Change*, Hampstead), Stephen Mangan as Goldberg (*The Birthday Party*, Harold Pinter Theatre), Ian McDiarmid as Shylock (*The Merchant of Venice*, Almeida), Sheridan Smith as Fanny Brice (*Funny Girl*, Menier Chocolate Factory). This is not a criticism of these actors, but a question aimed at the authenticity of apparent Jewish performances.

But no one took it seriously. It got no—and this is important—social media traction. Without that, you can forget outrage. All the main progressive movements of the past few years have come about because of the deeper democratization brought by social media. #MeToo, #OscarsSoWhite, #StopFundingHate, #BlackLivesMatter, #TakeAKnee—as demonstrated by the placement of the hashtag within their names—could not have happened without social media. All righting of wrongs happens online: no celebrity apologizes, no political leader sacks an underling wrongdoer, no corporation comes clean about malfeasance, unless they are under pressure to do so by the viral calls of Twitter.

The campaign to raise awareness around the casting of non-Jews in *Falsettos* did not go viral. I did not see #Jewface or #FalsettoGate trend on Twitter. There was no outrage anywhere on the internet.

If their attention is brought to it, progressives may not disapprove of the raising of the *Falsettos* case; but they won't get behind it. They won't step in, in the way they would if this was a play that had characters of color, gay, trans, disabled, autistic, or any other minority, portrayed by the wrong actors. To shake up privilege, you need the privileged: you need them to feel ashamed. You need the privileged, white, straight, cis-gendered, able-bodied to feel shame and anger on behalf of the minority that's being in some way traduced by them. And the privileged, white, straight, cis-gendered, able-bodied majority never feel these things when the minority being traduced is Jews; because they think that Jews are just ... them. They don't see enough difference.

Actually, it's not quite true that there was no internet outrage over *Falsettos*. On *The Stage* website, in the comments section below where the letter was posted, there was a fair amount of outrage—at the fact that the letter had been written at all. A Jimmy Murphy said, "Trying to conflate 'Jewface' with 'Blackface' is appalling. They need to withdraw that remark immediately if they are to be taken seriously." Another commenter, Ce Zar, said, "If I watched a play with let's say German actors portraying French revolutionaries I wouldn't mind as long as it's done well." And another, Paul Clarke: "[I]n the history of theatre, film and showbiz in general, you can hardly say that Jews haven't been significant or lacking a platform—literally, or behind the scenes, and countless have performed overtly, or covertly, over the years under gentile names." What you have here, beyond the sense of surprise and annoyance that any accusations of antisemitism engender, are some basic misconceptions about Jews. The second comment relates non-Jews playing Jews to Germans playing French people. Which is to imagine that Jewish is a nationality, not an ethnicity. The last one has a few more stereotypes in it—"Showbiz is so Jewish!"—and says that Jews, far from being discriminated against, have "performed overtly, or covertly, over the years under gentile names"—which is to suggest that Jewish actors changing their names was something Jews did as a secret operation to colonize the industry undercover, not a thing they had to do, because of racism: because a WASP audience would accept a star called Kirk Douglas, but not one called Izzy Danielovitch.

The first comment, which is the angriest, brings us back to the hierarchy of racism. Blackface is more offensive than Jewface. In fact, it's an insult to the importance of blackface to even invent the concept of Jewface.

But is it? The two racisms become confusingly conflated when *The Stage* prints the word "Jewface."

Anti-Black racism is the motherlode. The racism suffered by Black people is the one that shapes antiracist discourse. Blackface therefore is the default offense, and all similar offenses follow from it, and use the same construction: yellowface, brownface, redface—even drag has been described as womanface. All these bad faces are—to state the obvious—recognizable on the face. They involve makeup. Which brings us back to something about Jews: they aren't necessarily instantly recognizable as Jews. So how can Jewface be a thing?

Let's look again at some of those previous examples of non-Jews playing Jews. In *Hunters*, Al Pacino doesn't wear any kind of obvious Jewish makeup when he plays Offerman (except a beard, and little glasses, and his costume, a black rabbinical suit). What he does instead is play the character *really fucking Jewishly*. His performative mannerisms are full of shrugs and schlemiel-faced tics, his intonation pitted with melancholic question marks.* That's what Jewface is. We shouldn't really

---

* A wrinkle has appeared with this point, which is that—spoiler alert—in the final episode of *Hunters* it's revealed that Pacino's character is not Jewish. He's an ex-Nazi himself who has been pretending to be Jewish to become a Nazi hunter, all part of exorcizing his guilt. When I discovered that, I was going to cut this bit. Then it occurred to me that it's a very generous—and very meta—reading indeed of Pacino's performance to imagine that his employment of stereotypical Jewish mannerisms as an actor was a deeply buried clue to the fact that the character isn't actually a Jew.

use that blackface-inspired construction, because that implies makeup. But an actor can imitate without makeup. It's JewVoice, JewExpression, JewStoopedandShruggingBody. It's NebbishBeing.

Which is when this becomes really problematic: when you cartoon the Jewishness, and you yourself are not Jewish, what is that if not minstrelsy in another form?

Similarly, in 2019, I went to see the Regent's Park Theatre's new production of the musical *Little Shop of Horrors*. The part of the Jewish shop owner, Mr. Mushnik, was played—very well—by the Scottish actor Forbes Masson, but again, this character is stereotypically Jewish: all his gestures are New York shrugging and oy-ing. Having a non-Jew do those things is—if you follow the same logic that would apply if this was a Black, gay, trans, disabled, or any other minority character playing up stereotypical aspects of that minority—disrespectful to Jews.

This is partly the fault of Jews, by the way. *Falsettos* was written by Jews, and like all theater and comedy written by Jews about Jews, it is self-deprecating and not—as theater and comedy about other minorities and/or women tends to be—empowering. Here are some lyrics:

> JASON: In case of smoke, please call our mothers
> on the phone
> And say their sons are all on fire

MARVIN AND WHIZZER: We are manipulating
   people and we need to know
Our worst sides aren't ignored
MENDEL: The guilt invested will in time pay wisely
WHIZZER AND JASON: We do not tippy toe
WHIZZER: We charge ahead to show
MENDEL: We're good in bed

This is how the Jews have always portrayed themselves
(at least until Sacha Baron-Cohen appeared, but he's a bit
more Israeli, I think). The default Jew, in the Woody
Allen/George Costanza out of *Seinfeld* model, is a Nebbish:
an intellectual, klutzy neurotic.*

Actors who are playing Jews—at least Jews like the
ones in *Falsettos* and *Little Shop of Horrors*—they're not
really playing Jews as individuals. They're playing Jews as
stereotype. They're at some level making fun of Jews.

The progressive idea that you should only cast minority
actors to play those minorities has a two-fold motivation.
It is partly an employment issue, a push-back against a
previous open-to-all tradition that meant there was less

---

* Comedy nerds may interject: George is Italian. Yes, but in name
only. He is the character in *Seinfeld* most based on the very Jewish
creator of *Seinfeld*, Larry David. But when the sitcom was first
developed, NBC—antisemitically—felt that *Seinfeld* was Jewish
enough having Jerry Seinfeld at the center of it. So David and Seinfeld
dealt with this restriction by making George Italian, and Elaine a
WASP, and just carried on writing them Jewish.

work for minority actors. But it is also, and I would say at its core more so, about respect. There is something disrespectful, the reaction against Halle Berry and Scarlett Johansson suggests, about casting a cis actress in a transgender part. Just as a particular racism can only really be defined by the victims of that racism, the deep truth of identity is only available to those who live that identity. Casting a non-minority actor to mimic that identity feels, to the progressive eye, like impersonation, and impersonation carries with it an element of mockery: or at least, it is reductive, lessening the complexity of that experience by channeling it through an actor who hasn't lived it.*

All of that applies to Jews too, or at least it should. The Jewish experience is a lived one, and a complex one. Yet non-Jews *have* been allowed to play those parts that express the most complex sections of Jewish experience: Ben Kingsley is not Jewish (or at least, like Tom Rosenthal,

---

* A very clear indication of this was spelled out in a *Guardian* interview in 2021 with the deaf actress Marlee Matlin, which ended with her saying: "Enough is enough. Deaf is not a costume. It's not authentic and insults the community that you're portraying. Because we exist, we deaf actors. We do a much better job of portraying characters, telling stories that involve deaf characters, because we lived it. We know it." Matlin's point is still to some extent about employment—about those job opportunities for deaf roles going to deaf actors—but ringing out even more clearly is the sense—*deaf is not a costume*—that a hearing actor playing deaf is essentially an impression of a deaf person, and an impression of a deaf person by someone who can hear feels, to the deaf, insulting.

he actively disavows any trace of that heritage) and yet he plays Itzhak Stern, the Holocaust survivor who assisted Oskar Schindler, in *Schindler's List*. It's a great performance, but so is his Oscar-winning role in *Gandhi*, which *is* now considered problematic because, despite his half-Indian heritage, Kingsley wore makeup to make himself look darker. If it is problematic for a non-minority actor to portray the experience of a minority, it is problematic for all those actors listed in that letter to *The Stage* to play Jews, and for non-Jewish musical theater performers to sing songs like "Four Jews in a Room, Bitching" in *Falsettos*.

While we're on the subject of blackface vs Jewface: another #JewsDontCount moment happened while I was writing this book. The film director Ken Loach was made a judge of a school competition run by Show Racism the Red Card, which is a football antiracist charity similar to the aforementioned Kick It Out. In 2016, during an interview at the Labour Party conference, Loach said, on being asked about the presence at a fringe meeting of a speaker alleged to have questioned the history of the Holocaust, "Well, I think history is there for us all to discuss." He has since very strongly refuted being a Holocaust denier, but nonetheless this appointment led to protests from the Jewish community. For a while, *SRtRC* reacted angrily, doubling down, getting the legendary French soccer player Eric Cantona to tweet about what a great antiracist

Ken Loach was, and suchlike. In the end, Loach did step down from judging the competition, but as ever there was no outcry from progressive quarters—only Jewish ones—about the possible incongruity of his appointment.

I wouldn't particularly mention this—it's just a standard, everyday example of #JewsDontCount—were it not for the fact that while this minor furor was going on, a man called Dave Rich, who works for a charity, the Community Security Trust, which provides security against racist attack for Jewish schools, synagogues, and community centers, tweeted this:

Followed by a second tweet that just said: "I can think of better judges for an anti-racism competition." I retweeted it. And then Ken Loach's son, Jim, tweeted this:

Jim Loach @
@JimLoach

I see @Baddiel casually retweets internet trolls like
@daverich1 who defame my father @KenLoachSixteen.
You'd think with his background he'd be a bit more
careful when accusing others.

Which is me, in costume and makeup as the Nottingham
Forest soccer player Jason Lee, in a sketch from the show
Fantasy Football League, from the mid-nineties.

So. As I have said before, the makeup and costume in
that sketch were extremely ill-judged and a mistake. The
sketch was about Jason Lee not scoring, and was making
fun of him as a soccer player. But, however much it might
have felt OK to me and my co-host Frank Skinner at the
time to depict Lee by comically exaggerating his look, as
we did for many other soccer players lampooned on the

show, being made-up in that way has antecedents in a very bad racist tradition. We shouldn't have done it, and I have apologized for it publicly on various occasions since.

What the apologies make no difference to is the recurring presence of that photo on my Twitter timeline. Particularly since I started speaking out publicly about antisemitism, whether it be antisemitism in general or on the left. In fact, it can seem that what the people demanding apologies from me want is not apologies. What they seem to want, really, is silence. They want me to shut up, particularly about antisemitism. As far as they are concerned, the photo of me as Jason Lee is a trump card that means I cannot speak about racism, even the racism that threatens me personally.

It is suggestive, perhaps, of the hierarchy of racisms that because I was made-up as Jason Lee, I, a Jew, have no right to speak out about my experience of anti-Jewish racism. I have offended against the more important racism, and so I have no right to speak about my own— less important anyway—one.

There is a tactic some of you may be aware of called Whataboutery. Whataboutery is a charge laid against someone who might be trying to divert attention from their own wrongdoing by pointing out wrongdoing elsewhere. For example, people who are more concerned to defend Israel than I am often say, to those attacking it, why aren't you talking about human rights in Saudi

Arabia, or the persecution of Uighurs in China? And they are then accused of whataboutery. The accusation means: you are using this comparison to move the discussion away from the present arena because you feel defensive about it. Thing is, in the case of this book, it is impossible to talk about anti-Jewish racism without comparing it to other racisms; it's impossible to talk about how Jews are treated by progressives without comparing it to the way other minorities are treated. So I'm nakedly embracing whataboutery. Comparison is inevitable, because this book is about why things are different for Jews. So, to illustrate further how racism against the Jews is deemed less important than other racisms—and knowing full well that the whataboutery charge card is waiting for me—let's talk about *Bo' Selecta!*.

Bo' Selecta! was British comedian Leigh Francis's very funny Channel 4 sketch show, broadcast in the early 2000s, in which Francis dressed up as celebrities in grotesque cartoon masks. In a recurring sketch he portrayed me as a rabbi. Well, not just a rabbi, a Chasidic rabbi, with a massive nose, and curly hair, and a big black hat, who continually says the word Jew. Given my previously referred to outness as a Jew, I don't think this is unfunny, or, in a comically exaggerated way, inaccurate. But I do think, given that Francis is not Jewish, that it is racist—at least *as* racist as me dressing up as Jason Lee. This is not an attempt to excuse me dressing up as Jason

Lee (which was racist). It is an attempt, like everything else here, to note the difference in the reaction. I can guarantee that anything I say on Twitter, particularly anything about antisemitism, will lead someone, somewhere, to post that photo of me as Jason Lee, with a demand that I shut up and hang my head in shame. I have never seen, and expect never to see, any kind of condemnation, on the internet or anywhere else, of Leigh Francis for dressing up as Rabbi Dribbling-Screaming-Jew Baddiel.*

* * *

---

* In fact, during the height of the Black Lives Matter protests—and while there was much reaction in the U.K. to the use of blackface in British TV comedy in general—Francis did apologize: about his impersonations of Craig David, Mel B of the Spice Girls, and other people of color. But not about his impersonation of me.

A phrase I used in that last bit, "hierarchy of racisms," is troubling. I have noticed recently that if, in online discussions, I suggest that some microaggressions toward Jews would lead to a far greater outcry if perpetrated against another minority, sometimes I am told that this comparison is invidious: I remember being told once that in so doing, I was throwing the other minority under the bus. This, of course, is not my intention (although as we know, intention matters not very much anymore). I am arguing not for another person's experience of racism to be lessened in significance but for the awareness of something similar happening to Jews to be heightened.

But what that reaction—"you're throwing us under the bus'—suggests to me, really, is that by comparing another minority's experience of racism to that of Jews, I am belittling it. Because a Jew's experience of racism can't be that bad. Sometimes I use the phrase, on being told, as a Jew, how much worse racism is for people of color, "it's not a competition." But I use this knowing that for many, it is: that there *is* a hierarchy of racisms and some *are* more important than others. In fact, some see the competition as being slanted *toward* Jews. There are many who feel that, for example, what they see as the primacy, in the European and American imagination, of the Holocaust over other atrocities—slavery, or the Bengal famine—represents a feeling that a genocide happening to white people (and Jews are, of course, in this Schrödinger's

75

Whites-observed example, white) is somehow more important.

I also note the phrase "it's not a competition" being thrown back toward me when I say, as I have done a few times on social media, #JewsDontCount. But that is to misunderstand what #JewsDontCount is trying to communicate. It is my position that racism should not be a competition: that all racisms should be regarded as equally bad. "Should" is the key word here. There is *an* inequity, even if that inequity may be felt differently in different quarters. For example, some Muslims feel strongly that Islamophobia doesn't get the attention that antisemitism receives in the news media in general. But this polemic is very specifically about progressives: it's not about the mainstream media. And it's written from the point of view, to use a phrase much beloved of progressives, of my lived experience: the lived experience of a Jew who feels as most Jews do that the reaction of progressives, to antisemitism, is that it doesn't matter very much.

Indeed, from some progressive quarters I perceive in recent times not just that antisemitism doesn't matter very much, but that, as a concern, it's been tainted; that it's become, as it were, *their*—the other side's—racism, the one *they* care about. In October 2020, a freedom of information request by the Union of Jewish Students revealed that only 29 out of 133 universities across the UK and Ireland had adopted the International Holocaust Remembrance Alliance's definition of antisemitism, and that 80 of them said they had no current plans to do so. According to *The Times*, some said that it was "not necessary" (a phrase that perhaps serves, in its dismissiveness, as an objective correlative of the title of this book). Meanwhile, in the more progressive *Guardian* the focus was less—was absolutely not—on the element of Jews not counting than on the fact that the Conservative government got involved. The education secretary, Gavin Williamson, sent a letter to vice-chancellors expressing unease about the lack of interest from universities in applying the IHRA's definition, particularly given the recent general rise in antisemitic incidents on campuses. The *Guardian* piece on the subject ended with these two paragraphs:

> Williamson's intervention comes at a difficult time for many universities struggling to cope with hundreds of students and staff infected with Covid-19, as well as preparing for the UK's exit from the EU and its impact on recruitment and funding.
>
> "When future historians look at the Covid-19 period, there will be a complete mystification at what the Department for Education took to be a priority in the middle of the crisis," said one university official.

Note the reference to history, and the certainty about who and what is on the right side of it. Note also the element of irritation, of institutions being bothered by this trifling issue when there are so many more important things to worry about. But note mainly, "Williamson's intervention": concern about antisemitism comes from the right.

This is all echoed on social media. I see many posts now suggesting that, for example, when the Conservative Party raises Cain about offenses against Jews but ignores Islamophobia in its own ranks, it marks antisemitism as the favored racist issue of the right. Similarly, when a right-wing provocateur, such as the Northern Irish ex-politician David Vance, posts racist tweets, they aren't just condemned for doing so: there is always, now, an outcry about how Twitter is clearly biased because it has not suspended this tweeter from the platform yet it takes swift action against anyone accused of antisemitism, such as the British rapper Wiley. The suggestion is that Wiley was made an example of when he posted a series of anti-semitic tweets in 2020 because he was Black, but also because Jews are treated, by the powers that be, as a special case. Except this isn't quite true. Twitter started taking this kind of action only fairly recently, as an upping of its game against hate speech. So although Vance had indeed been tweeting offensively against a number of minorities over the length of his time on the platform, since Twitter has been reacting like this, he was in fact removed—following outrage over a tweet he sent in September 2020 to the Black soccer player Marcus Rashford—just as quickly as anyone else. But the idea persists that Wiley was suspended faster, because Jews are somehow protected by power, privilege, and wherever—in this case a social media giant—the money is.

A very clear example of the deeply problematic and contradictory currents around the idea of a hierarchy of racisms in progressive circles came when the *Guardian* columnist Hadley Freeman wrote a piece for the newspaper entitled "After Wiley, I Didn't Have a Fight On My Hands for Once. Why Did That Feel So Weird?" The premise of the piece was that under usual circumstances, raising one's voice publicly about antisemitism leads to various progressive condemnations—references to Israeli oppression, insistences that other minorities have it worse, and so on, but this in fact had not happened to Freeman when she had spoken out about Wiley online. Implicit in this piece is the assumption that antisemitism is low on the hierarchy of racisms, which is why she was expecting those responses. It might be seen as an advance that the article did not get them: except that it did. Not from readers, but, it later emerged, from other contributors to the *Guardian*, some of whom tweeted that they felt the newspaper should not be publishing a piece implying the existence of a hierarchy of racisms—and that to suggest that anti-Jewish racism is not taken seriously enough might be to suggest that other racisms are taken *too* seriously. Which is a complaint I've already addressed, the Catch-22 that Jews in asking for parity with other racisms are seen to be minimizing the effect of those racisms, so should just shut up about it, really. Interestingly, though, a few days after Hadley Freeman's piece was published, the *Guardian* put out another article, this time entitled "'Hierarchy of Racism' Fears Threaten Starmer's Hopes of Labour Unity" in which the central angle was the concern of progressive Labour members that recent decisions by the new party leader were creating an impression whereby "antisemitism was seen as the most serious form of prejudice, while Islamophobia and anti-Black racism were considered less important." So. A hierarchy of racisms clearly *is* an issue for progressives: as long as it is that way round.

For a long time, only Jews really cared about Jews, only Jews really cared about antisemitism. Now that antisemitism can sometimes seem like a right and left issue, I perceive the emergence of a particularly modern form of antisemitism, which is an association of *anti*-antisemitism with Establishment values. Saying "this is antisemitic" for some, puts you firmly into the camp of the oppressor. People who think this, however, forget that the notion that Jews control the hand of the oppressor puts them in the Kevin Strom camp.

* * *

Meanwhile, I think it is the case that there are certain times in history—during the 2020 Black Lives Matter protests, for example—when the fight against racism and discrimination directed toward one particular minority has to be given prominence. But, despite the vital ground-shaking antiracist change those protests spurred forward, there were problematic issues at their margins for Jews. For instance: in June 2020, after a spate of statues associated with slavery were torn down, the American activist Shaun King tweeted: "Yes, I think the statues of the white European they claim is Jesus should also come down. They are a form of white supremacy. Always have been. In the Bible, when the family of Jesus wanted to hide, and blend in, guess where they went? EGYPT! Not Denmark. Tear them down."

Then, in July 2020, following the general questioning around race and ethnicity provoked by BLM, the Archbishop of York, the Right Reverend Stephen Cottrell said, in the *Sunday Times*, "Jesus was a Black man." This led to much debate, such as an article on Forbes.com entitled "Was Jesus Black or White?" that leaned heavily toward Jesus being Brown-skinned, which he no doubt was.

But in the article, as in Shaun King's tweet, or Reverend Cottrell's interview, the one racial identity that the historical Jesus is fairly universally accepted as being was not mentioned. His Jewishness wasn't part of the discussion, and felt, in the answer to this question, irrelevant. It felt, in fact, erased.

The move to reclassify Jesus as non-white is good and historically accurate. The erasure at the same time of his Jewishness is neither. It accords in fact with centuries of the Church doing the same. Some might argue that the re-imagining of Jesus as a Brown-skinned Middle Eastern doesn't exclude his Jewishness. Theoretically, of course, it doesn't. But the reclaiming of Him* as non-white, in truth, bypasses that, because it has no political impact, no revolution, to reiterate Jesus's Jewishness. The truth of this is clear in King's need to highlight, from the life of Jesus, a Gospel story that is only in Matthew, the flight to Egypt. He could have said, if he wanted to make it clear that Jesus was not from Denmark, that he lived and preached and was crucified in Judea: in the Middle East land of the Jews. But he doesn't want to do that, because that is not, in his eyes, to remake Jesus away from being white. To reiterate Jesus's Jewishness does not, to Shaun King, do anything for his blackness. In fact, in aggressively insisting that a new Jesus of color needs to be affirmed, the identity "Jew" is thrown in, as it so often is, with whiteness. It elides Jews with the generalized

---

* As we know, I'm an atheist, but I'm going for the capitalization as it makes who I'm talking about clearer, I think.

privileged category that this new radical Jesus needs to be prized away from.

Similarly, if less aggressively, in August 2020, a poet called Omar Sakr tweeted this image created by the photographer Bas Uterwijk:

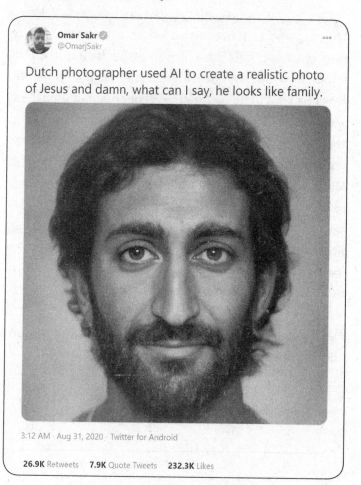

Omar Sakr ✔
@OmarjSakr

Dutch photographer used AI to create a realistic photo of Jesus and damn, what can I say, he looks like family.

3:12 AM · Aug 31, 2020 · Twitter for Android

26.9K Retweets   **7.9K** Quote Tweets   **232.3K** Likes

You may notice this has gotten a lot of likes and retweets, meaning, on Twitter, approbation. People like this. They like it because it reclaims Jesus. It says, Jesus was stolen by white people, and now we're setting the record straight and bringing him home.

I think that's a positive thing to do. However, Sakr is a Muslim, who says that Jesus, like this, looks like family. And although this idea doesn't specifically exclude Jews—there are of course Arabic Jews, and Jews and Muslims tend to be of the same genetic Abrahamic heritage—I checked the responses, of which there are many, and couldn't see one that mentioned Jews. I couldn't see one that said "At last, an image of Jesus as he really was—a Middle Eastern Jew." The point being that the reclamation of Jesus as non-white is a party to which Jews—certainly, Jews perceived of as white—are not invited. Or to put it another way: I look at that picture, and damn, he looks like family to me, too. But I know I would only be trolled on Twitter for saying so.

Meanwhile, in July 2020, an American actor and personality called Kevin L. Walker tweeted this:

Kevin L. Walker ✓
@KevinLWalker

Fact:
Jewish people migrated to "Hollywood," founded & created it, milked black people for their #culture, & music, and catered to the KKK and racism in America.

They deliberately created a social system putting black people at the bottom.. Thus the role we're mostly cast in.

5:50 PM · Jul 16, 2020 from Los Angeles, CA · Twitter for iPhone

He went on in this vein for a while. It's a classic example of racism against Jews being cast as punching up: as speaking out against the Man. It's probably worth mentioning, by the way, that this is not a #JewsDontCount example. This is straightforward, active antisemitism. The #JewsDontCount side of it is that there was very little progressive calling out of Walker for it. And Twitter, a site that you can be ejected from for accidentally misgendering a trans person, issued no suspension or even reprimand.

Unfortunately, there has always been a not much talked about—because it presents an uncomfortable issue, especially for progressives—history of antisemitism within a section of Black activism. Among the many great things Malcolm X said, he also said:

> But let's not forget the Jew. Anybody that gives even a just criticism of the Jew is instantly labeled antisemite. The Jew cries louder than anybody else if anybody criticizes him. You can tell the truth about any minority in America, but make a true observation about the Jew, and if it doesn't pat him on the back, then he uses his grip on the news media to label you antisemite.

Which is a fairly classic example of the high-low duality: the Jew is at once absurdly powerful and yet a child who cries louder than anyone when criticized. However, the high is more important, because it clothes the speaker in the robes not of racism but revolution. When Wiley launched that series of anti-Jew statements on social media in the summer of 2020, he was not, in his mind, attacking a minority but, in that tradition of Malcolm, expressing a rebel yell, a shout-out against power. I did an interview in response on Times Radio saying that "there hasn't been anyone with such an enormous platform coming at Jews in such a blatant way before," and Wiley said: "'Cos everyone was scared that's why."* So it's not just a shout-out, it's a *brave* shout-out—Wiley isn't a racist, he's a hero, finally standing up and saying the things that need to be said even though it will bring down the wrath of this all-powerful Jewstablishment on his head.

Perhaps the most extreme example of this is Louis Farrakhan, the leader of The Nation of Islam, who continues to have the support of some sections of the Black activist community, despite saying that Judaism is a "gutter religion" and "Hitler was a very great man." But let me be clear about something. Farrakhan gets into trouble for this. He is called out for it by progressives, and his brand of extremism is not in general supported by them.†

---

* Wiley also said, "David Baddiel come and talk to my face." Also, "Emma Barnett get me on your show." And said something about Alan Sugar that I can't now find on the internet. It began to remind me—this is really a joke for football fans—of the Norwegian commentator who when England lost to Norway started listing all the famous English people he could remember in order to convey his sense of triumph. "Winston Churchill ... Lady Diana ... Lord Beaverbrook, your boys took one hell of a beating." I could kind of hear Wiley in his head going "David Baddiel ... Emma Barnett ... Alan Sugar ..." but then running out of any more Jews he could think of, despite us infiltrating and owning the entire media.

† Although just before this book went to print, there was an op-ed piece in the *New York Times* entitled "The Woman Behind the Million Man March" whose agenda was taken by some Jews as an attempt to rehabilitate Farrakhan. When the issue of potential Jewish offense was pointed out to the author, academic Natalie Hopkinson, she tweeted, "Somehow among a million concerns, you believe that yours are

Yet no one says to Farrakhan, as they do, for example, to me because I wore blackface in a sketch once, that he now has no right to talk about the racism that affects his own community. In other words: progressives will criticize Farrakhan and Wiley and other Black activists for antisemitism. But they will not tell Farrakhan and Wiley that because of their anti-Jewish racism they can't now speak about anti-Black racism. Only offending against one type of antiracism can lead to cries for the cancellation of your ability to speak about racism at all.

Similarly, during the fallout from the Wiley rant in the U.K., I noticed some people saying that they were uncomfortable with Jews going on the radio and criticizing Wiley when those Jews hadn't done enough to help the Black community stand against racism in their struggle. This struck me as quizzical, but instructive. While it is undoubtedly the case that standing with the Black community against racism is a good thing to do—and many prominent Jews have done it, the history of civil rights, particularly in America, is in fact full of cooperative outspoken support from Jews and Jewish groups—I

---

supposed to rise to the top. That is called privilege"; and in a second tweet, "Ppl who have become white should not be lecturing black ppl about oppression." Which is perhaps the best example I've ever seen of Schrödinger's Whites, from the point of view of a progressive observer: a progressive observer who sees no problem with telling Jews not just what they are, but what they have mutated into.

don't understand why, in speaking out against racism toward one own's minority, it's a *requirement*. Or at least, it's not a requirement that works the other way round. As is often the case when you apply that reversal with Jews, it begins to sound comical. But I'll put it forward anyway. I can't imagine anyone saying, of a prominent Black person about to go on the radio and speak about Black Lives Matter, "Hang on—what have they done recently to help Jews in their struggle against antisemitism?"

At the heart of this lies the already mentioned flickering whiteness of Jews. It is a stone-cold progressive trope that inverse racism does not exist: that, because of the power structures that western culture is built upon, it's not possible for a Black person to be racist about a white person, and crying inverse racism indicates mainly that the person crying is themselves a racist, or, at least, displaying White Fragility and White Privilege simultaneously. This has value as an idea, but hits a problem with Jews. If Jews are assumed to be white, then of course what Wiley or Malcolm X, or even Louis Farrakhan, are saying isn't racist. Indeed, Wiley's confusion, as I saw it, on being called out for his antisemitism was partly about that. It seemed to me that Wiley at some level just thought: What's the problem? I'm just having a go at some white people. And we're allowed to do that.

Which is why, in order to remind people that Jews *are* a minority, and *do* suffer from racism, one has to—*I* have to—use the trope of "let's examine how this would feel if it happened to any other minority." For example, while we're talking of Black Lives Matter: just before she left the Labour Party, at the end of 2018, the MP Luciana Berger collated a series of online examples of antisemitic hate directed at her ("Are you still after the £1m reward bounty posted by Israel then Luciana? I wouldn't bother, they won't pay up," or "Israeli shill," or "How many shekels?"). I replied by calling on progressives to see the racist abuse of Luciana Berger as equally bad as the racist abuse of a person—a politician—of color: the then Labour Shadow Home Secretary Diane Abbott. I was immediately put right by various progressives about how the abuse was not equivalent, and of course not antisemitic:

Replying to @Baddiel

Wrong as usual. This is nothing to do with her ethnicity. Berger is being called out because she's a member of the shady Labour Friends of Israel. Same thing happens to the many non-Jewish LFI members - Ryan, Streeting, Gapes, Woodcock (when he was still Labour) et al.

12:59 AM · Dec 14, 2018 · Twitter Web Client

I expected that. But then Diane Abbott herself posted:

Which, obviously, I agree with. But I noticed something else about her response. Abbott had taken the antisemitism—indeed, the whole issue of racism—away. My point was that Luciana Berger's hundreds of examples of antisemitic abuse shown in her tweet should garner the kind of reaction from progressives that a similar collation of anti-Black abuse would. Abbott's post then broadened the issue of racist abuse to that suffered by women in public life generally.

This is exactly the same tactic that the right employ when they try to counter the #BlackLivesMatter movement by saying #AllLivesMatter. The sentiment might sound virtuous and true, but really it's just an attempt to widen the focus of the debate so as to lose the specificity of Black concerns. As has become clearer recently, there are particular and pressing dangers involved with being Black that all people do *not* have to deal with, and the statement #AllLivesMatter is simply a bad faith way of blanketing over that. Similarly, in Luciana Berger's post, there were examples of anti-Jewish racism that all women do *not* experience. And in making this about *all* women, Diane Abbott was neatly sidestepping the antisemitism.

Which is a process I perceive as always there when the left are forced to deal with antisemitism. As, for example, when Jeremy Corbyn himself and his supporters defend themselves from the charge of turning a blind eye to it. What they tend to say is: *we stand against antisemitism and all types of racism*. As a mantra, this was heard again and again between 2015 and 2019, and continued to be in the ongoing arguments around Corbyn. It sounds good. It sounds right. But to these ears, the reflex need always to follow the phrase antisemitism with "and all types of racism" is the left's All Lives Matter.

What about Israel? Isn't Israel *actually* an oppressor? Aren't most of these books about the new Jew-hatred actually about Israel, and how the left's hatred of that country spills over from anti-Zionism into antisemitism? Well, yes, they are, but I kind of think: Fuck Israel. I call Israel, on Twitter, stupid fucking Israel, which tends to upset some Jews, but it isn't really a comment on the country itself. It's more to do with the debate, the way that everything anyone says about that subject so quickly gets drawn into the stupid fucking shouting match. Or indeed *not* about that subject. Here's a typical Twitter moment from my timeline:

For a long time online I used to hand out an award for this sort of tweet, called the #BringIsrael PalestineIntoItSomeFuckingHow Award. Then I realized it was happening so often it was pointless.

For those who might be wondering, my position on Israel is: I don't care about it more than any other country, and to assume I do is racist. To assume that I have to have a strong position either way on Israel is racist. Because I am a British person—a Jew, yes, but my Jewish identity is about Groucho Marx, and Larry David, and

Sarah Silverman, and Philip Roth, and *Seinfeld*, and Saul Bellow, and pickled herring, and north London seders, and my mother being a refugee from the Nazis, and wearing a yarmulke at my Jewish primary school—and none of that has anything to do with a Middle Eastern country three thousand miles away. And also: Israelis *aren't* very Jewish anyway, as far as my relationship with Jewishness is concerned. They're too macho, too ripped and aggressive and confident. As I say of them—or, to be precise, Lenny, a Jewish-American taxi driver character I invented for my film *The Infidel*, says of them—"Jews without angst, without guilt. So not really Jews at all."

Some people feel this is a callous attitude, that I should care more about the Palestinians. I do care, but not more than I care about the Rohingya, or people suffering in Syria, or Yazidi women, or starving children in Burkina Faso. I care about all these things but not enough, because if I did—if I were a better person—I would give up my luxurious life in London and go help some of these people. But as I am not that person, the idea that I should care *more* about the Palestinians smacks of something weird. It smacks of an idea that somehow Jews—non-Israeli Jews—must apologize for Israel: that Jews—non-Israeli Jews—should feel a little bit ashamed of Israel, and must, before they are allowed into any kind of public conversation, make some kind of supplicant-like statement to that effect.

I think, by the way, that a lot of Jews on the left *are* ashamed of Israel, and so they go out of their way to say so. Fine. I'm not suggesting that the state of Israel hasn't done many things to be ashamed of. But here's the thing: I am not responsible for those actions and expecting that I should feel so is racist. If a non-Israeli Jew does feel responsible, it is *internalized* racism. To be perfectly honest, I think a fair amount of Jews on the left are just ashamed of being Jewish. I think Jews on the left have to some extent absorbed the myths about Jews being rich capitalist power mongers, and so therefore make a special point of how un-Jewish they are, the objective corollary of which is hating Israel. Me, I think, Israel? Meh.

The above was written before the outbreak of violence in Gaza in May 2021. My basic position hasn't changed, but I'm writing this American edition in the midst of the extreme reactions on all sides to the re-igniting of that conflict, and there is something I'd like to add. Which is, weirdly, about Jesus again.

There was a Free Palestine demonstration in London in May 2021 too. Many of the protesters were carrying placards. A lot of these had Nazi and Holocaust references on them, but the one that got to me had an image of Jesus on it—quite nicely drawn, reminiscent of Christian comic strips I remember from my childhood—carrying a cross, pictured at one of the stations on the way to the crucifixion. And underneath it were the words: "Do Not Let Them Do the Same Thing Today Again."

Even though, as I said above, I try and avoid doing so, it is difficult, sometimes, when you're talking about antisemitism not to be drawn into the conversation about Israel-Palestine. The drawing-in normally takes the form of a long angels-on-a-pin debate about the "difference between anti-Zionism and antisemitism." This debate stretches from, on the one, conservative Jewish hand, saying there is no difference, to the other, modern progressive hand, saying there's a wide gulf between the two and the personification of anti-Zionist protest as antisemitic is just a way of smearing it as racist to discredit pro-Palestinian activism.

For me, if I'm forced to talk about it, the distinguishing between the two is actually quite simple: look for the ancient trope. One of the things about antisemitism is: it's a very old racism. There are bad myths and bad imagery and bad associations that antisemites have been applying to Jews for centuries, for long before 1948, when the state of Israel was established. If these are found within a political conversation about the present-day Middle East, then my anti-Jewish racism radar goes off. There are many other markers that people who want to have this debate all the time bring to it, notably the intense focus on Israel-Palestine compared to many other conflict areas and outrages happening elsewhere in the world, but for me the trigger is in the history, in noticing if the negative thing being said has always, not just now, not just since 1948, been said about Jews.

So. That placard is not, like other stuff I've talked about on these pages, a complex bit of antisemitic code. It doesn't sneak past you. It's the oldest negative myth about the Jews, older even than the blood libel or Jews secretly controlling the world: Jews are Christ-killers. Let's not get into the complex theological history of this (obviously it was actually the Romans who killed Christ, plus the death of Christ is clearly crucial to the salvation of humankind anyway, so surely whoever "killed" Jesus are key players in that sacred narrative ... OK, I have got into it), because the unmistakable message of that myth is: the Jews are murderers, murderers of all that is good and innocent and sacred in this world.

Now, you may, if that is your politics, want to say this of the Israeli government. And you could proclaim this of the Israeli government and make a case for that utterance not being an antisemitic statement. But "Them" on that placard doesn't mean The Israeli Government. To requote Toby Ziegler: it means Jews. It expresses the eternal and recurring wickedness of Jews. It must do, as Benjamin Netanyahu, however much of a devil you think he is, was not around in AD 33 cheering for #TeamBarabbas.

97

I perceive, though, in the recent stronger-than-ever reaction to the conflict in the Middle East, a weakening of this always weak border between the "acceptability" of anti-Zionism versus the unacceptability of antisemitism. One of the singular features of this particular racism, including the way it is viewed by avowed antiracists, is an underlying suspicion that antisemitism does not arise, like all other racisms, spontaneously from the hatred and scapegoating of the majority culture, but from something perpetrated by the minority itself: what the left in other contexts, but not in this one, calls victim-blaming. Hence when bad things happen to Jews, Jews are always, in some way, responsible. The activist Tariq Ali, speaking during the same march that the Jesus placard was seen at, said: "Stop the occupation, stop the bombing and casual antisemitism will soon disappear." I'm not entirely sure if by casual, Ali is including, as happened in London in the same period, a convoy of men in cars calling through bullhorns, virtually in earshot of my house, for the rape of Jewish wives and daughters. Either way, the notion that the wellspring for antisemitism is simply the actions of the Israeli government is ahistorical in the extreme. Some fairly big antisemitic events did in fact happen before 1948—in fact, in one quite notable case, very recently before then.

For a long time, antisemitism has been downgraded as not a real or proper racism by progressives. Now, in the social media-inspired frenzy, which demands villains, who must have justice meted out to them immediately, things have moved beyond that. The idea that collective responsibility is racist has got lost in the righteous fury. Any Jew is fair game. As I was writing this, a British-Lebanese blogger told her 11k followers to come and harass me on my stand-up tour, because the proceeds from my book are no doubt going to fund illegal settlements and Israeli Defense Forces killing. In L.A., diners at a Sushi restaurant were interrupted by protesters demanding to know which ones were Jewish. The news in the U.K. showed pictures of two activists who went to Golders Green—a Jewish area of north London—then put up screens depicting Holocaust images, and holding microphones aggressively approached Jewish passers-by insisting they renounce Israel (despite the fact that many Orthodox Jews refuse to believe in the state of Israel anyway).

If something similar had been perpetrated in a Muslim area of London, this action would've been shut down immediately and widely condemned by progressives. But there is a sense now that antisemitism is understandable. In a documentary I made for BBC 2 called "Confronting Holocaust Denial," Professor Gilbert Achcar of the School of Oriental and African Studies at the University of London told me that the prevalence of Holocaust denial in Gaza and the West Bank—about 80 percent of people there subscribe to the conspiracy theory—needs to be understood as a reaction to their circumstances, an irrational fighting back against something held to be sacred by the enemy. Which is fine as a piece of analysis, but it's complicated if you take understandable to mean, as it often does, *excusable*. Huge increases in attacks on Jews—600 percent in incidents in the U.K. alone over this period—seem to be met with a shrugging sense that there's something appropriate about that. Somewhere in the hive mind, certainly as you can hear it buzzing on Twitter, is a sense that Jews experiencing violent pushback, wherever they are, and whatever their views about this conflict with which they may have no connection, is fitting. This is bad for Jews, obviously, but it also bad for the many, many people who support the Palestinians while wanting to have no truck with racism against Jews.*

---

* Even people whose job it is to protect and educate the wider world about anti-Jewish racism are presently falling into these traps. Literally as I was writing this, I saw in the news that in Austria a non-Jewish woman had been assaulted on a train by three men for reading a book called *The Jews in the Modern World*. The police chose not to charge the men, claiming that her doing so at the current time was "provocative." An academic called Daniel Landau, described in British newspapers as "an education expert commissioned by the government to create antisemitism awareness training for Austrian police," went on Austrian TV and said: "It's like telling a woman who has been raped 'why did you dress so provocatively?' It must be made unmistakably clear that reading a book in this country does not constitute complicity." That second sentence is odd. It is a good analogy, from the point of view of improving progressive

#JewsDontCount has many historical antecedents. A memo given out by the British Ministry of Information in 1940, an instruction to its own propagandists, suggested that the idea of atrocity—what it calls "horror"—"must be used very sparingly, and must deal with the treatment of indisputably innocent people: not with violent criminals, and not with Jews." This instruction came from a number of beliefs. Primarily, it came from a sense, prevalent in the government of the time, that the British public should not feel they were fighting a war on behalf of the Jews. But underneath that is something deeper. Underneath that is a profound belief that Jews do not belong in the category of the indisputably innocent: that, just by virtue of being Jewish, they have sinned. The memo displays the belief that to get behind a fight

understanding of antisemitism, to compare the attackers' defense to that of rapists who talk about women dressing provocatively. But the word *complicity* rings alarm bells. Complicit with what? Who? Jews? And if reading *was* a complicit act, and therefore made this woman complicit with Jews, would the attack therefore have some justification? Because reading could be seen as a complicit act: I might feel provoked if someone was reading *Mein Kampf* on the London Underground in front of me. But this woman was simply reading a book about Jews. If you extend the analogy, a woman who rapists suggest was dressing provocatively would never be accused, by progressives, or hopefully anyone, of being complicit with anything—because the complicity implied could only be with the bad imagination of the rapist. But there is a suggestion in Landau's words that the bad imagination of the attackers on the train might have some validity if the woman involved was actually identifying with Jews by reading this book.

against terrible injustice, ordinary British people need to feel that that injustice is 100 percent unjustified: and who can believe that, really, about the Jews?

To put it another way: Jews are not in the sacred circle. They aren't quite worth protecting. The same slip,* whether it be Freudian or otherwise, was made in 1980 by the French prime minister at the time, Raymond Barre. Following an attempted terrorist bombing of a synagogue in Paris, Barre described it as "a hateful attack which wanted to strike at the Jews who were in that synagogue, and which struck innocent French people who were crossing the street." Which means that somewhere in Barre's subconscious those Jews who were the target of the attack were not innocent: and also, not French.

And then there are people for whom the slip is perhaps not a slip. Until February 2021, Jenny Tonge sat in the House of Lords. She was originally a Liberal Democrat, although after a series of antisemitic statements she was finally ejected from that party. During Jeremy Corbyn's

---

* I don't wish to let light in on magic here, but while redrafting this book, my editor wrote in the margin, "Are we calling the previous example a slip?" I thought about this for some time. I see that her point is that calling the sentence in the MOI memo a slip seems to minimize something potentially horrific, but at some level it's the *mot juste*. In fact, it's sort of the *mot juste* for what I perceive as the problem that this whole book is wrestling with, which is a set of unconscious assumptions about and attitudes toward Jews that slip out and often, most significantly, slip in as well.

time as leader of the Labour Party she became a supporter of his. She posts regularly on her Facebook page. For example, very soon after white supremacist Robert Bowers' massacre of Jewish worshippers in Pittsburgh in 2018, she posted:

Jenny Tonge
1 hr ·

Absolutely appalling and a criminal act, but does it ever occur to Bibi and the present Israeli government that it's actions against Palestinians may be re-igniting anti Semitism?
I suppose someone will say that it is anti Semitic to say so?

HAARETZ.COM
Eight killed in Pittsburgh synagogue shooting; gunman yelled 'All Jews must die'

To which I replied that it was "fucking antisemitic to say so." Which was perhaps less temperate a response than that of the Palestine Solidarity Campaign, an organization to which Tonge belonged but stepped down from soon after her post. The PSC said in a statement that "while the post acknowledged that the killings were appalling and a criminal act, it risked being read as implying that antisemitism can only be understood in the context of a response to Israel's treatment of Palestinians. Such a view risks justifying or minimizing antisemitism." This is an insightful statement. It points out something key about antisemitism, which is a deep resistance to the idea of it as what you might call a stand alone racism. The Jews must always be in some way responsible. If it's not bankers and capitalism, it's Israel.

Jenny Tonge didn't really listen, though, to the Palestine Solidarity Campaign. Soon after that post, she doubled down. On August 11, 2019, in response to a video posted by a woman from New Zealand entitled "Why I'm a Zionist," she wrote:

 Jenny Tonge shared a video. •••
August 11 at 9:27 AM · ⊙

This is excruciating to listen to. Self justification, complacency, manipulation of 'history'. Just sickening.
We would all like a safe haven to run to when the going gets tough, but we stay on and ask why it is getting tough. Why have the Jewish people been persecuted over and over again throughout history. Why? I never get an answer. If we discussed this we would be accused of anti Semitism, so better not, and so it goes on!

I posted:

>  **David Baddiel** ✓
> @Baddiel ₀ₒₒ
>
> And meanwhile I'd like to know why Jenny Tonge, a Lib Dem peer in the House of Lords - the Lib Dems btw, have always had their fair share of anti-Jewish racists - can say this and retain her seat there, as the implication of her question *is* just straightforward Nazism.

One of the things about being a non-Zionist is it puts you in an interesting position with left-wing antisemites. Most left-wing antisemites assume that you're only using the cry "antisemitism!" because you're a Zionist. Since I'm not a Zionist, this is confusing. Although it shouldn't be, of course, if what I'm doing is crying "antisemitism!" because I've seen something antisemitic.

The antisemitism is fairly apparent in this case, I would say; not even hiding in plain sight. Avowed anti-Zionists such as Tonge, in order to avoid accusations of antisemitism, are normally careful not to use the word "Jews" or "Jewish." Even the conspiracy theorist David Icke tends to religiously use the phrase "Rothschild Zionists" when he means Jews. So it's quite surprising that she drops "the Jewish people" into this post. More: the Jewish people "throughout history." As we know, Israel has not existed throughout history. So what she's talking about here is clearly an eternal condition, a default setting, of the Jews.

Tonge's implication in her question—"Why have the Jewish people been persecuted throughout history?"—is that there must be some reason for this persecution, and the fault lies with the Jews. It's what we now call victim-blaming, although that isn't a term that, say, Adolf Hitler would have been familiar with when he claimed in *Mein Kampf* that the Jew "was only and always a parasite in the body of other peoples." By the way, to find that quote, I went to a random chapter of *Mein Kampf* and put in to the search engine the word "always"—because the one thing I know about antisemitism is that the antisemite believes the Jew never changes, which is the reason they might be persecuted throughout history.*

Some could say that Tonge was asking a good question, which is: what is the *external* reason for this throughout-history racism against Jews? To which the answer might be that all majority cultures need to have an alien hate object, and for Christian cultures, in particular, that position has long been filled by Jews. But I know that this

---

* Always watch out for *always*, from antisemites. A central Nazi propaganda film was called *The Eternal Jew*. A more recent example has been Roald Dahl, who in 1982 said: "There is a trait in the Jewish character that does provoke animosity. Maybe it's a kind of lack of generosity to non-Jews. I mean, there's always a reason why anti-anything crops up anywhere. Even a stinker like Hitler didn't just pick on them for no reason." Which is not, again, a #JewsDontCount example. The #JewsDontCount example is that in the U.K. we celebrate Roald Dahl Day, with hardly a tremor.

is neither the question she is posing, nor the answer she wants. I know that the question Tonge says she'd like answered is not one about the psycho-social power structures that perpetuate racism against Jews but: *what is it that the Jews do—always, eternally, throughout history—to make themselves so eminently persecutable?* And that the answer—the unsayable answer—she so desperately claims to want ("I never get an answer!") is in fact one she has absolutely at the ready, and it's an image in her head not dissimilar to the mural that Mear One painted on that wall of Jewish bankers playing Monopoly on the backs of the world's poor.

You can also feel the lower idea of Jews, as sickening vermin, coming through in Tonge's post.* I hadn't previously watched the video that provoked her to this point, but I just have, to see what was quite so sickening about it. It's a Jewish woman from New Zealand, fully aware, as most Jews now are, of how reflexively bad a thing a Zionist is assumed to be, explaining why she nonetheless is one. Even though I'm not a Zionist, I was not sickened by it. I didn't agree with it. But I was not sickened by it.

---

* One thing about the low part of the antisemitic, high-low duality is that the image of Jews that comes with it is always weak and contemptible but never victimized. In the double-sided hate, the low-ness of Jews is that they are hideous and irritating and repugnant, but this is just a condition of being Jewish, it is not forced upon them.

And I have repeated the word sickened enough times now to make my point, I hope, clear: Jenny Tonge's response was, to use a word the anti-Zionists use a lot, disproportionate.

Her response is visceral, it is physical: the video makes her feel sick. Her response is one of disgust: disgust with Jews, for both manipulating history (high status) and for snivellingly wanting a safe haven to run away to (low status). Disgust with Jews for failing to be the tough that get going when the going gets tough (like, y'know, when you're being herded naked at gunpoint with your children into a mass grave that you dug yourself).

This disgust is what drives Tonge into the silence, the silence at the heart of the Facebook post. For anyone still in any doubt about what she means, her imagined frustration at not being allowed to speak truth to Jewish power— "we would be accused of antisemitism!"—is where, to quote Bono, she gives herself away. Because it would not be antisemitic to ask the question: why are majority cultures always in need of a minority to fear and loathe? What is it in the psychosis of the mainstream that requires Emmanuel Goldstein and his Two Minutes Hate? It can only be antisemitic to ask the other question, the question which is not a question but just a statement of hate: what is it about the Jews that makes them so hateful?

And then, just to confirm that this *is* what Jenny Tonge means, I got this tweet in response to mine:

> **▮▮▮▮▮**   ⚬⚬⚬
>
> Replying to @Baddiel
>
> But that is a fair question!! Why?
> You always brings nazi everytime the questiom arise.
> You even bring Nazi while killing Palestine. Why?
> The next generation will think Holocaust is a scam by
> Zionist.
> Better make more Evil Nazi movies fast!
>
> 2:43 PM · Aug 18, 2018 · Twitter for Android

It's difficult to know who ▮▮▮▮▮ is. She presents also as a person of color, and a Muslim, I think from Indonesia, but it's entirely possible that her real name is Sergei and she works out of a basement in St Petersburg.

But let's assume for the moment that she's real. It's hard to deconstruct her tweet, because, obviously, she doesn't quite speak English and, obviously, she doesn't quite speak Logical. But she is doing something that aids *my* logic, which is drawing out the not-so-latent racism in Jenny Tonge's post. She did this most effectively in her continued conversations with others:

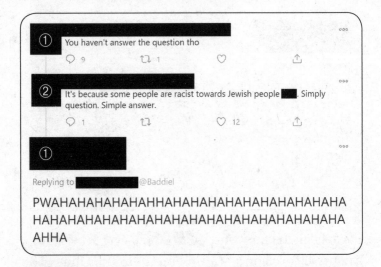

You haven't answer the question tho

It's because some people are racist towards Jewish people ███. Simply question. Simple answer.

Replying to ███ @Baddiel

PWAHAHAHAHAHAHAHHAHAHAHAHAHAHAHAHAHA HAHAHAHAHAHAHAHAHAHAHAHAHAHAHAHAHAHA AHHA

███████, you see, isn't so bothered as Jenny Tonge was with discretion, and therefore with silence. She doesn't need to worry about being accused of antisemitism, and therefore is happy just to laugh in the face of an accusation of it. More profoundly, she just thinks that the idea that Jews might suffer racism is itself laughable. Which again is useful, as it can be spooled back to fill Jenny Tonge's silence: the sense that Jews are powerful and in control and therefore oppressors means that discrimination against them can't be taken seriously and isn't, in ████████'s mind, even really possible.

It's changing. The omission of Jews from identity politics is not quite what it was. Late in 2020, for example, the Roald Dahl estate apologized for Dahl's antisemitism (see footnote, page 106). This was in line with the kind of public apologies for various offenses against various minorities that are now a regular occurrence in the culture. The word, however, that needs to be shaded in a little there is not "apology" but "public." The apology came to notice only when, in the U.K., the *Sunday Times* unearthed it, because it was buried in a difficult-to-find part of the official website. As the newspaper put it, "to find it from the home page of Dahl's official website, one must scroll down to the bottom, click 'About us', then choose to 'Find out more about the Roald Dahl Story Company', the little-known corporate entity that runs his literary estate. You must then click on 'RDSC and family notice', which does not mention the words 'apology', 'antisemitism' or Roald Dahl." Which makes it a different kind of apology to the more performative all-over-social-media sort that guilty white public figures regularly now employ in the hope that it will exculpate them from other kinds of historic racism. Moreover, the very same edition of the *Sunday Times* included a big article about an upcoming TV Christmas family drama, *Roald & Beatrix: The Tail of the Curious Mouse*, which suggested that Dahl's heart-warming reputation in the U.K. would somehow stay intact.

It remains uncertain how far Jews themselves are prepared to go to create the level playing field. On December 1, 2018, Giles Coren, who is the restaurant critic for *The Times*, and Jewish, reviewed the Ivy Café in St John's Wood, an affluent and fairly Jewish neighborhood in north London. He began the review by saying that three times in recent memory he had sat with other foodies, other critics, who were not Jewish, and who had, in talking about this restaurant, called it the Oy Vey Café.

Giles mentions this at the start of the review, and then frets. He frets about whether or not he should have said something. He frets about whether or not it is racist. He frets about whether or not the people making the joke knew that he was Jewish. He basically goes into a tizz along the lines of THEY HATE US, AND LET'S NOT MAKE A FUSS ABOUT IT. I posted that he should "name and shame the racist fuckwit. The time of Jews laughing along with this shit and thinking offense against us doesn't matter like it does to other minorities is over."

This was, to some extent, bravado. I don't know that it is over. I don't know that Jews are now prepared to make the same sort of fuss as other minorities. But between 2015 and 2019, the branding of the Corbyn Labour Party as antisemitic had the effect of politically mobilizing, for the first time, the British Jewish community. Which also, for the first time at least since World War Two, brought in a wider community. Antisemitism as an issue got noticed. There were articles about it in non-Jewish newspapers; politicians got asked difficult questions about it on the

TV; there was even a hashtag—#enoughisenough—that may or may not have trended for a bit on Twitter.

It was also, of course, a branding massively resisted by many on the left, including Jews of the left. As I said earlier, the progressive idea that it is the prerogative of those experiencing racism to say "this is racism" was not complied with by every single British progressive during that time. What happened instead was that large parts of the left* indulged, from the word go, in the very un-progressive act of victim-blaming (as well as whataboutery: "What about Islamophobia in the Tory Party?" etc). No doubt there *were* examples in the very long toing and froing of accusations and defenses around the issue of Labour Party antisemitism where the Jewish community overreacted. No doubt also there was much weaponization, by Labour Party enemies, of the issue. Let's have a look at one example of that weaponization.

Matt Hancock, the British Health Secretary, was filmed speaking before the 2019 election at his own constituency. He got into some trouble over the Conservative manifesto pledge to supply the National Health Service

---

* There is an online thing, called #notallmen or #notallwhites—which is a satirical hashtag. #Notallmen, for example, is often placed by feminists after something critical of the patriarchy because they know that if they accuse "men" of doing something, men online will reply excusing themselves from this accusation. Similarly, in this case, obviously, I'm aware that this behavior I'm describing needs the qualifier #noteveryoneontheleft.

with fifty thousand new nurses. The crowd became restless. Desperately he reached for a trump card: Labour Party antisemitism. It was a cynical, panicky move. But the crowd's reaction is, to my ears, astounding. On hearing Hancock's pledge to "fight the antisemitic racist attitudes of Jeremy Corbyn," the crowd boo him, they swear, they get up, and take the mike from him. I then noticed footage of it all over social media, much of it posted positively by progressives, often with jokey headlines like "Scenes." So I posted:

David Baddiel ✓
@Baddiel

The upbeat, jocular RT'ing of this vid by progressives...hmm. Hancock is a Tory twat, playing the anti-Semitism card here in a crass way. And yet: my ears still found the baying of the mob, on hearing the word anti-Semitism, terrifying.

Immediately, I got a lot of progressive fury back at me. Here's one of the less furious ones:

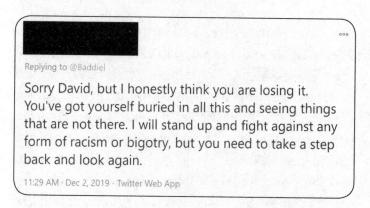

Sorry David, but I honestly think you are losing it. You've got yourself buried in all this and seeing things that are not there. I will stand up and fight against any form of racism or bigotry, but you need to take a step back and look again.

11:29 AM · Dec 2, 2019 · Twitter Web App

This includes the pledge "I will stand up and fight against any form of racism or bigotry." Which is an interesting thing to say while dismissing a Jew who has said he is frightened of the noise a mob is making once triggered by the word "antisemitism." Here's another:

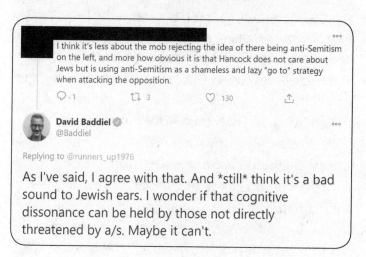

I think it's less about the mob rejecting the idea of there being anti-Semitism on the left, and more how obvious it is that Hancock does not care about Jews but is using anti-Semitism as a shameless and lazy "go to" strategy when attacking the opposition.

David Baddiel
@Baddiel

Replying to @runners_up1976

As I've said, I agree with that. And *still* think it's a bad sound to Jewish ears. I wonder if that cognitive dissonance can be held by those not directly threatened by a/s. Maybe it can't.

What I'm doing there, perhaps, is reaching out to ███████████, and people watching my conversation with ███████████, under the assumption that they will recognize that what they can't factor in, in their understanding of this, is the lived experience of Jews. I thought by making clear my own vulnerability, using words like "threatened" and "terrifying," people would understand that I'm presenting a complex, perhaps contradictory, idea: I'm aware that Hancock is playing antisemitism as a card, but that awareness is overridden by the pure sound of a mob reacting scornfully, and dismissively, and violently, to the word "antisemitism." Whatever the context, however crass Matt Hancock is being, that sound, to Jewish ears (and most Jews agreed), is frightening. I think what was never understood by those in the Labour Party who became defensive around the issue of antisemitism between 2015 and 2019 is how scared, at base, Jews are. Jews, particularly those of my generation, were brought up under the shadow of the Holocaust. My mother was born in Nazi Germany. I only exist by the skin of my teeth.

Yeah, yeah: the Nazis. There is, I think, among those who would be dismissive of antisemitism a fair bit of Nazi fatigue. Godwin's Law is an internet adage that states: in any online argument, eventually, someone will analogize what is being discussed to the Nazis, at which point the discussion will be over. I agree that it's best, debate-wise, to avoid comparisons with the Nazis. I've noticed, though, that sometimes people don't realize that there is one exception to this rule. Here is someone called ████, not realizing it:

David Baddiel ☑ @Baddiel · Oct 18, 2017
OK. Really wish you'd have been there to politely point out to the Gestapo who killed my atheist great-uncle that he can't have been a Jew.

100% agree with ████████. If you're an atheist then you can't be a Jew. And perpetuating 'Jews are different' causes antisemitism.

💬 63   🔁 522   ♡ 2.7K   ↑

Replying to @Baddiel

Great, let's use Nazis to frame the argument. Always a good approach.

What ██████ hasn't realized is that when you are talking about antisemitism, it is always OK to refer to the Nazis. Because it's not like debating veganism and then calling someone Hitler because they drink milk. With antisemitism, the one thing *is* the other. Jews have this reference point, a terrible one, but intellectually an inescapable one. We have the advantage—weird word, but I can't think of a better one—of having an objective corollary of what happens when antisemitism is allowed to run unchecked.

But still: I sense the *yeah, yeah.* The historian Deborah Lipstadt, when I interviewed her for a BBC 2 documentary about Holocaust denial, talked about something she calls softcore Holocaust denial, which would include, and I quote, "Yes, but look at you now." Meaning: come on Jews, you're OK now. You're rich, you're powerful, you've got Israel. Basically, it's non-Jews saying, enough already. I see it, very subtly, in Ash Sarkar saying "at this point in history" in the sentence "Antisemitism, at this point in history, is primarily experienced as prejudice and hostility towards Jews as Jews, largely without aspects of material dispossession." In one very simple way of course, Sarkar is right: Jews, in general, are not now having their assets stripped from them in the way they were during the 1930s in Germany. But that is to imagine that history does not live both in the memory and in the culture. I was born nineteen years after the war ended. As I grow older, nineteen years feels like yesterday. The dispossession and trauma experienced by my grandparents didn't end with them. My grandfather was in and out of a mental hospital for the rest of his life with clinical depression. My mother was an amazing woman, but deeply damaged. And as for me ... well, that's another book. The point is, history is not past. Its effects live in the present.

But for those who do, still, think *yeah, yeah, enough already*, I said earlier that being white was not just about skin color, but about security. That's what white privilege represents. White really means: safe. How safe do Jews feel right now? Well, here's a table from an E.U. report published in 2018 that surveyed Jews living in Europe about their level of concern regarding various types of antisemitism (the numbers given indicate the percentages of Jews who agreed that these things were worryingly present in their respective countries):*

	AT	BE	DE	DK	ES	FR	HU	IT	NL	PL	SE	UK	Av
Antisemitism on the internet, including social media	85	92	89	71	86	95	81	90	80	92	81	84	89
Expressions of hostility towards Jews in the street or other public places	46	81	80	47	52	91	46	51	71	37	69	52	73
Antisemitism in the media	51	84	68	51	85	80	69	73	63	73	63	61	71
Antisemitism in political life	63	69	61	37	66	67	74	55	49	77	58	84	70
Vandalism of Jewish buildings or institutions	31	68	61	45	45	88	35	48	57	39	60	45	66
Antisemitic graffiti	36	64	53	28	54	83	58	66	38	71	48	45	64
Desecration of Jewish cemeteries	40	53	61	20	31	83	53	51	37	51	48	45	63

I'd say those are fairly high percentages of things that, as a Jew, I would consider mark me out as not safe. Similarly, in 2018, 60 percent of all religiously motivated hate crimes in the United States were perpetrated against Jews (by contrast 18.6 percent targeted Muslims). I don't like

---

* And here are the countries represented by the abbreviations:
AT = Austria, BE = Belgium, DE = Germany, DK = Denmark,
ES = Spain, FR = France, HU = Hungary, IT = Italy, NL = Netherlands,
PL = Poland, SE = Sweden, UK = United Kingdom.

statistics much, though—hard to garner any reality from them—so here, from 2019, are a collection of specifics that might give that sense of unsafety more of a visceral reality:

In Paris, a student was beaten unconscious on the subway for speaking Hebrew on his phone. During the Yellow Vest protests in the city a writer and philosopher was set upon by crowds shouting "dirty Jew" and "dirty Zionist shit." In Berlin, a teenager was strangled by three men shouting antisemitic abuse at him. On Yom Kippur, a gun-wielding man tried unsuccessfully to enter a synagogue where approximately eighty congregants were worshipping. After the failed attempt, the gunman shot at nearby individuals, killing two and wounding two others, none of whom was affiliated with the synagogue. In London, a rabbi was hospitalized after being attacked by two teenagers yelling "Kill Jews." Near where I live, in Belsize Park, shops were daubed with Stars of David and the legend 9-11. In Melbourne, a Jewish boy was forced to kiss a classmate's shoe. In Poland, a Jewish cemetery was vandalized with the words "Jews eat children." In Amsterdam, on Bevrijdingsdag, the national holiday commemorating liberation from the Nazis, a Jewish man was assaulted by revelers singing songs about gassing Jews. In Moscow, a yeshiva was set on fire. In Istanbul, a synagogue was firebombed. In Ukraine, rocks were thrown at the windows of synagogues. As the year came to an end, five Americans were shot and killed in a kosher grocery store in Jersey City.*

This—a handful of the total incidents—is why Jews don't feel white, if by white you mean safe. And as for me: I didn't feel white when, as a twelve-year-old at a new school, a teacher was overheard to say of me, venomously, "Jew," and another teacher replied: "Of course." I didn't feel white when, loving T.S. Eliot as a teenager, I discovered that he considered Jews to be lower than rats. I didn't feel white when I was being beaten up in London by skinheads in the 1970s, however much I might later convert it into comedy. I didn't feel white when a man behind me at Stamford Bridge shouted repeatedly "Fuck the fucking Jews!" I didn't feel white when I received furious tweets to tell me Mear One's mural isn't antisemitic, but, rather, justifiably shows "Zionist greed." And, as the examples of Jews not counting have built up, I haven't felt all that white writing this book.

---

* By the way: it used to be the case that while violence against Jews might be minimized or excused by some on the left, it tended still to be mainly perpetrated by the far right. Now—and I would say partly because of something this book is about, the positioning of Jews as privileged/on the side of the oppressor—it's not so simple. Some of these attacks will have come from the right, but some will have come from Islamists, and the Yellow Vests cover a wide political spectrum, including the far left. Meanwhile, the Jersey City shootings were carried out by two people linked to a group called the Black Hebrew Israelites. As a Jew, now, you can feel under attack from all sides.

A postscript. Anyone who does manage to read the 720 pages of Charlie Kaufman's *Antkind* may notice that the main character claims throughout that he is not Jewish. Does this invalidate my opening point?

Well, no. A lot of heavy lifting is being done in that sentence by the word "claims." The main character sits in the great tradition of unreliable narrators. He sees himself as extremely progressive, but in fact his thoughts and actions often give him away as the opposite. Similarly, via his regular protesting-too-much about his non-Jewish-ness, it would not be a radical reading to imagine that B. Rosenberger Rosenberg clearly is Jewish but like a lot of Jews, as discussed on these very pages, is conflicted and ashamed and in the closet about that. Indeed, he is conflicted and ashamed about his Jewishness partly because he knows Jews do not fit into the sacred circle that progressives have drawn, what he calls the "apple cart of hierarchical suffering" (which he is keen never to upset). B. Rosenberger Rosenberg is desperate, throughout the novel, to identify and sympathize with women, African-Americans, trans people, disabled people and others who *do* fit into the sacred circle—he often wishes to *be* a woman, African-American, transgender, or disabled—and yet his obvious ability to come out as Jewish is consistently ignored.

Like many Jewish utterances about Jewish identity, Kaufman's is complex and layered. It's one of the most important and significant recurring themes in *Antkind*. But it's not mentioned in the *Observer* review because, well, to use a well-worn phrase, it doesn't fit the narrative. Or to use a less well-worn phrase, because Jews don't count.

Coda

October 30, 2020

This is a pretty topical book, which is good and bad. Good that it's about a subject presently very much in cultural play, bad that the landscape is in the process of continually shifting. While I was writing this book, the Labour Party in the U.K. was being investigated for antisemitism by an independent body, the Equality and Human Rights Commission, and I'd literally just handed in the final draft when, on October 30, 2020, its report came out: and the left-wing shit hit the Jewish fan, or the other way round, depending on your point of view.

The report was damning, finding various evidence of anti-Jewish harassment and discrimination, and concluding that the party had failed to provide effective measures against "antisemitic conduct" in general. Jeremy Corbyn responded with a statement accepting some of the EHRC's findings but insisting that the scale of antisemitism in the party during his leadership had been

DAVID BADDIEL

exaggerated for political reasons. He was then suspended by the new leader, Keir Starmer, which led to intense anger from the left.

In terms of this book, some might say: so there you are—Jews count. Look at this enormous political fuss, about Jews. How can you say they don't?

Well, first, that's what it is: an enormous *political* fuss. With very little what you might call *people* fuss. For about five seconds, after the report came out, there was a sense of relief among British Jews that perhaps now the wider public would understand their fears and anxieties over the last five years: that, in other words, the effect of the report would be to bring into focus the *lives* of Jews and the real human cost of racism against them. But very quickly, as soon as Corbyn issued his statement, antisemitism became again what it's been throughout this process, a way of expressing not your feelings about the fragile lived experience of Jews, but your political affiliation. I saw statements posted online from prominent progressives, including MPs, to the effect that Corbyn's suspension was *clearly* an attack on the left. Those statements leaped very quickly over a lip-service acknowledgment of the seriousness of the EHRC report's findings, into an assumption that really, Jews, antisemitism, all that, was just a means to get rid of what remained of Corbyn's influence. It intensified what, as I've said in these pages, already existed, a bifurcation of the fight against antisemitism on political lines. To say, as Keir Starmer did, that he was committed to eradicating anti-semitism was seen, bizarrely, as a right-wing statement.

This has the effect, paradoxically, and despite all the noise around the issue, of making Jews—the real individ-uals caught in the cross-fire, that is—feel that they count even less than they did at the start. As, for example, a progressive Jew who might support the attempt to rid the Labour Party of antisemitic elements, it makes you feel like your reality doesn't figure in this fight at all. It makes you feel, in fact, like the people that are being fought about aren't you at all.

It also, I noticed, intensified the argument central to this book around the scratchy issue of the hierarchy of racisms, and whether such a thing exists and is allowed to be talked about. On the *Today* program on the day all this broke, Angela Rayner, the deputy leader of the Labour Party, said that Jeremy Corbyn was "a thoroughly decent man," but with "an absolute blind spot and a denial when it comes to some of these issues." I have used the words "blind spot" myself in these pages, and I don't think it's entirely wrong to use them to describe the progressive miasma around antisemitism: it's what I mean by passive as opposed to active. But the issue at this stage is not was Corbyn and the 2015-19 Labour leader-ship team actually antisemitic or antisemitic by oversight, but the progressive forgiveness of it *either way*. Not to put too fine a point on it, if Corbyn's blind spot was about racism toward Black or Brown minorities—or indeed, say, trans people, as the Labour MP Rosie Duffield could evince in the extreme and angry progressive reactions she has gotten to supporting J.K. Rowling against some of the attacks on her—I don't believe that any progressive would still be describing him, despite this, as a thoroughly decent person. We live in a culture where if someone notable sins against one of the modern progressive articles of faith, the rest of their work and character is not taken into account: it's all overridden, as they are, in the now tired parlance, canceled. It doesn't matter how clearly decent and valuable J.K. Rowling's work and life was before she got involved in the trans debate. Those who would condemn her do not say she is a thoroughly decent person with an unfortunate blind spot: she is now on the wrong side of history, an active transphobe, a bad person. Not being antisemitic, therefore, is not one of those articles of faith.

Or to put it another way. One of the previously mentioned journalists and commentators in this book, Hadley Freeman, tweeted on October 30, 2020:

> **Hadley Freeman** ✔
> @HadleyFreeman
>
> Question: would addressing bigotry against any other minority be seen as an unfortunate distraction from the bigger picture, or is it just antisemitism?
>
> 7:56 AM · Oct 30, 2020 · Twitter for iPhone
>
> **86** Retweets   **124** Quote Tweets   **1K** Likes

Soon after, another previously mentioned journalist and commentator, Ash Sarkar, tweeted, seemingly in response:

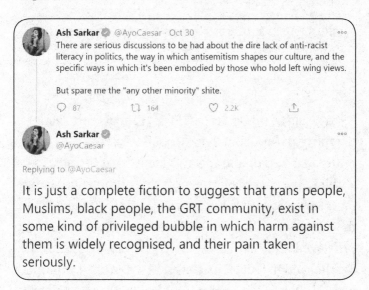

> **Ash Sarkar** ✔ @AyoCaesar · Oct 30
>
> There are serious discussions to be had about the dire lack of anti-racist literacy in politics, the way in which antisemitism shapes our culture, and the specific ways in which it's been embodied by those who hold left wing views.
>
> But spare me the "any other minority" shite.
>
> 💬 87   🔁 164   ♡ 2.2K
>
> **Ash Sarkar** ✔
> @AyoCaesar
>
> Replying to @AyoCaesar
>
> It is just a complete fiction to suggest that trans people, Muslims, black people, the GRT community, exist in some kind of privileged bubble in which harm against them is widely recognised, and their pain taken seriously.

In the strange world of Twitter, Sarkar's process is known as sub-tweeting, that is, drawing attention to someone else on Twitter without mentioning them by name, and it's entirely possible that this was continuing in Freeman's next tweet:

Hadley Freeman ✔
@HadleyFreeman

Replying to @HadleyFreeman

I was angry & hurt when I tweeted this so I will rephrase it more precisely:
Would addressing bigotry against any other minority be seen BY THE SELF-DESCRIBED ANTI-RACIST LEFT as an unfortunate distraction from the bigger picture, or is it just antisemitism?

9:33 AM · Oct 30, 2020 · Twitter for iPhone

So to be clear: this is a typical Twitter spat, and Twitter is not the real world, but it does, politically, refract a version of the real world, and the arguments that define it. And within what this book is about, this argument is important. Sarkar is, of course, correct. It is a complete fiction to suggest that all the minority groups she mentions are privileged and that their pain is forever taken seriously by the wider world in general. It is not a complete fiction—hence Freeman's qualification—that their pain and harm is taken more seriously *by progressives* than that inflicted on Jews. Sarkar herself does that in her already quoted article suggesting that contemporary Jews do not suffer, as other minorities do, from "aspects of material dispossession," which, whether it's true or not, suggests that she does believe in the existence of a privileged bubble for Jews.

But one other part of Freeman's response speaks to me: the reference to anger and hurt. This comes back to what I said earlier about the erasure in all this of the real experience of Jews. It's clear to me, clearer since I started writing this book, that if you suggest that progressives might operate an unconscious or otherwise hierarchy of racisms on which anti-Jewish racism is placed lower as a concern than others, you will be quickly accused, by progressives, of racism. Or at least, of minimizing the struggles of other minorities. At worst, there are shades in this accusation of Jews operating a typically Jewish (read, via Schrödinger's Whites, white) privilege, by insisting continually on their entitled place at the front of the pain line.

The point about this accusation is that it leaves Jews who *feel* the hierarchy of racisms—who see and hear it every day in the sort of examples that began this book that Jews don't count—nowhere to go. And: very many Jews are themselves progressives. This is at the very heart of Hadley Freeman, the *Guardian* writer's anger and hurt. Progressive Jews, Jews who would never want in any way to minimize the struggle of other minorities, are cowed from talking about their sense of not being cared for by their own comrades because of this. They feel cast out and alienated from their spiritual home, and they can't even express that for fear of being accused of racism.

There was another post on Twitter that brought this home to me in a more personal way. On the same—I'm tempted to say fateful, but that sounds a bit silly—day, the extremely distinguished British actor Robert Lindsay posted:

Robert Lindsay ✓
@RobertLindsay

I can't help feeling @jeremycorbyn has been severely maligned.
His political views in contrast to the current trend and his struggle with the media were never going to make him the PM but in comparison to the voices we are hearing now he certainly isn't racist

5:25 PM · Oct 30, 2020 · Twitter for iPad

1.1K Retweets   **195** Quote Tweets   **6.3K** Likes

A very well-liked tweet, as you can see. Various Jewish tweeters did object, cautiously, but Lindsay batted their concern away, saying that he could not "bear to see this man pilloried when we have the likes of Trump, Johnson, Farage and others fueling such hate and division."

Of course, one of the things about Trump, Johnson, Farage,* as far as progressives are concerned, is that they are racist. The fact that Jews might think the same thing about Corbyn was, clearly, for Lindsay, not to be taken seriously. But I don't want to just give another example of a progressive whose concern for most minorities' experience of racism does not line up with his or her concern for Jews. I want to tell you how this made me feel. Because when I was young, Robert Lindsay was in a BBC sitcom called *Citizen Smith*. It's what made him famous. He was totally brilliant playing Wolfie Smith, a young maverick left-winger who, though naively forever fighting for lost causes in 1970s lower-middle-class suburban London, was still a hero. He was definitely for this young, left-wing Jew also living at the time in lower-middle-class suburban London, a hero.

So obviously I know that was an actor playing a part. I know that was fifty years ago. But still, on realizing that for Wolfie Smith, Jews don't count, a tiny part of me died.

---

* I've had a note from my U.S. editor to explain who Nigel Farage is. Frankly, I think most of you know, as he hung around a lot with Donald Trump, and Trump brought him onstage at numerous rallies. Anyway, he's the man mainly responsible for Brexit. I'm really not going to explain what that is. There is a limit.

Acknowledgments

I'd like to thank for all their various help in the creation of this book: Rozalind Dineen, Stig Abell, David Roth-Ey, Myles Archibald, Iain Hunt, Ellie Game, Jean Marie Kelly, and Georgia Garrett.

Also from TLS Books

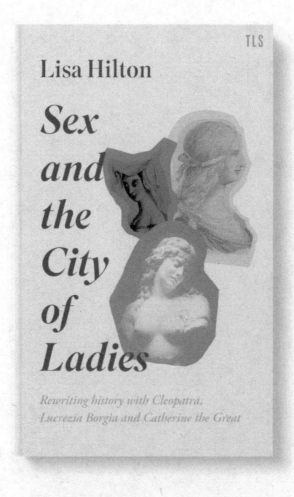

Lisa Hilton picks up the mythical 'City of Ladies' where the medieval writer Christine de Pisan left off, continuing a conversation about gender and greatness that began more than six hundred years ago.

Also from TLS Books

PATRICIA
WILLIAMS

GIVING

A

DAMN

RACISM, ROMANCE AND
GONE WITH THE WIND

TLS

How was the USA, the richest and most diverse nation on the planet, brought to the brink of resurgent violent division?

The answer begins with slavery.